I
MUST
KEEP
MOVING

DEMETRIUS MCCRAY

I Must Keep Moving: *Resisting the Urge to quit*

Published by: Demetrius McCray

Unless otherwise noted, all scriptures are from the KING JAMES VERSION (KJV): KING JAMES VERSION, public domain.

Copyright © 2019, 2024 Demetrius McCray

ISBN: 978-1-684542-98-7

Editing by Demetrius McCray
Front cover image by Marvin Eans
Book design (Interior) by Demetrius McCray

All rights reserved. No part of this book may be reproduced in any form or by any electronic or mechanical means, including information storage and retrieval systems, without permission in writing from the publisher, except by reviewers, who may quote brief passages in a review.

Printed and bound in the United States of America
First printing March 2019

This book is dedicated to the memory of my beloved father, Hubert McCray. He is truly loved and will be missed!

CONTENTS

FOREWORD

INTRODUCTION

Chapter 1: GO 1

Chapter 2: DEPARTURE 19

Chapter 3: UNEXPECTED CIRCUMSTANCES 29

Chapter 4: YOU'VE GOT A LOT TO GET RID OF . 41

Chapter 5: I MUST KEEP MOVING 55

Chapter 6: PERSEVERANCE BY FAITH 67

Chapter 7: PERSEVERING WITH INTEGRITY 79

Chapter 8: I'M GOING OVER 91

Chapter 9: MOVE ON 109

Chapter 10: GET A HEAD 129

DECLARATION 139

FOREWORD

God is a moving God. He is not an idol and he is certainly not idle. The God of the Bible and all of the universe is a moving God. He can be seen moving from the beginning to the end of scripture. In Genesis, the first book of the Bible, mentions that the "Spirit of the Lord moved upon the face of the waters." (Genesis 1:3). If God is water, he's living water (John 7:37-39). He's moving. If he is wind, he's a mighty rushing wind (Acts 2:2). He's moving. This concept even permeates to the very end of scripture where, in the final book of the Bible Revelation, the disciple John pens the words in Revelation 22:20 "He which testifieth these things saith "Surely I come quickly". Amen. Even so come quickly Lord Jesus". Undoubtedly, it can be said of God that he is in no way stagnant but always moving, manifesting, and working.

If movement is an attribute of God, and a part of God's nature then it should most certainly be a part of ours. After all, we were created in the very image and likeness of God. All of the profound parts of our lives physically, emotionally, and spiritually depend on movement. I recently read an article that began with the words "Sitting will kill you". The article began to explain the incredible benefits of movement in regard to health. The same is true spiritually. Sitting will kill you. We are called to keep moving at all costs. This is what the psalmist David was speaking to in Psalm 23:4 when he declared "Yea, though I walk through the valley of the shadow of death, I will fear no evil". In this iconic line of Scripture, David was letting us know that his posture in even the toughest and terrible of times would be walking. In other words, David said I will not live in, what God has called me to walk through. Despite the lowness, loneliness, and darkness of life's valleys you simply must keep putting one foot in front of the other. Sometimes the only resolve you must maintain in life is that you must keep moving. In fact, if you can keep moving, God promises a prepared table on the other side for you, a fresh anointing, and an overflowing cup (Psalm 23:5). You must keep moving.

Unfortunately, many simply do not make it to the table, receive the anointing, or find the overflowing cup because they give up somewhere in the valley. In other words, most never make it, because simply they stopped moving. However, I think the reason behind stopping is deeper than dark valleys. Many stop, quit, or maintain because they simply misunderstand progress. Somewhere along the way, we classified progress as jumps, leaps, and runs. But progress cannot begin to stride until it first finds the value of a step. See, progress, at its root is movement, no matter how big or small, in the right direction towards the right destination. Is it possible that some stop because they simply don't see the value in their last small step?

God understands the power of a step and its ability concerning movement and progress. God so values steps that he "orders them". Psalm 37:23 tells us that the steps of a good man are ordered by the Lord. God knows how to take a good man's, good or bad steps, and order them in such a way that they ultimately end up in the place God desires them to be. Never underestimate the power of the smallest step. Small or large, God is in the "steps" business. It is God's desire for you to make it. Can you trust God with your next step? It's God's desire for you to fulfill your purpose. You cannot quit, and you mustn't stop. You must keep moving. In fact, if you don't quit, you can't be stopped! God has designed your purpose to prevail all you need is a step in the right direction.

I believe that this is the very reason you haven't quit yet. I believe that this is the very reason you're holding this book. You know you're not finished, and that God is not done. Sometimes in the journey, all you need is a nudge. Sometimes all you need is a small shove to get yourself started again. Prepare to be pushed! "I Must Keep Moving" is what you have been waiting on.

If that is your desire, my spiritual son, Demetrius McCray, has written just the book for you. Demetrius, through the leading of the Holy Spirit, has written the book to do more than get you back on your feet, but rather a book that will get your feet back to moving. His unfolding revelation in each chapter and upon each page will incite a hunger for God's purpose for your life. The principles Demetrius gives within this book bring practicality and application that allows you to do more than read this book but live out this book. Getting back on track could be just a read away.

Quitting is easy and destiny, at times, can seem unreachable. But if you'll just keep moving your purpose is closer than you think.

Josh Carter
Pastor, Author, Evangelist

Introduction

I am writing this book because I believe that life is a journey and we take journeys within the journey. A Journey is the process of going from one place to another. With every journey, there is a starting point and a destination.

In the Bible, life and the journey to obtaining a goal or reaching a destination are sometimes talked about in the context of a race. Hebrews 12:1 says, "Let us run with *perseverance* the race that is set out for us." At the start of a race, an announcer addresses the runners with the words "on your mark." That is the starting point. In Philippians 3:14, Paul says, "I press toward the mark." That is the destination or goal. After reading these verses, the Lord made it so clear to me. On any journey there are two marks, there's a mark we begin on and there's a mark we end on, yet life happens in between.

A journey isn't just making geographical moves, it can also be an emotional, spiritual, mental, or physical journey. Not everyone's journey looks the same because our experiences aren't always the same. However, I do believe that there are certain experiences that most of us have in common. I'm a firm believer that there is always wisdom that can be extracted from our experiences. When we go through times of difficulty and we learn how to overcome certain obstacles, then we are able to help others get through similar situations. Our experiences build our credibility so that we are able to help other people *persevere* when they feel the urge to quit in the middle of their journey.

Every circumstance that I've faced and everything that I've gone through up to this point in my life was necessary for what I am about to share with you in this book. I have learned that life happens. Some things will be within our control and there will be things that are beyond our control. Though life may happen, we should never allow any trial, circumstance, tragedy, or difficulty to steal our intentionality. What do I mean? Just because life happens, it doesn't mean that we should passively allow life to dictate the quality of our journey. When we choose the plan of God for our lives and allow him to order our steps, life doesn't become perfect, but we have what we need to persevere through any circumstance.

In this book, I use several biblical events and characters to share with you the wisdom I've extracted from those experiences as well as my own. I pray this book helps enhance your journey and that you will reach your destination, become all that God desires you to be, do all you were created for, and possess every promise with your name on it! When life happens in the middle, you must tell yourself "I Must Keep Moving!"

Chapter 1
GO!

"Now the LORD said to Abram, "Go from your country and your kindred and your father's house to the land that I will show you."

-Genesis 12:1

"On your mark," a command used to tell runners to get into position for the start of a race. Your mark is never outside of your lane. God will never give you a beginning that gets in the way of someone else's. Whenever God positions you, he positions you to begin, to start, set out on a journey. The journey called destiny isn't some average or common thing. God doesn't position you to stay, he positions you to start. The starting place isn't the staying place. As you're reading this book, I believe that there is something deep down inside of you that's telling you it's time to GO! Go get your degree, start a business, write a book, reconcile with a family member, or even better your physical health. It's time to begin your journey! Go!

Abraham, who is known as the father of faith, doesn't come from a family that worshipped God, he comes from a family that served other gods. "And Joshua said to all the people, "Thus says the LORD, the God of Israel, 'Long ago, your fathers lived beyond the Euphrates, Terah, the father of Abraham and Nahor; and they served other gods" (Joshua 24:2). No one in his family was a priest, preacher, missionary, prophet, deacon, or anything that has to do with God. However, Abraham's background didn't stop what God saw in him. He saw a man of great faith, a man who would make history, a man who would change the world. Despite your background, your history, your economic status, or even the color of your skin, God sees great potential in you!

The Apostle Paul says, "But by the grace of God I am what I am, and his grace toward me was not in vain. On the contrary, I worked harder than any of them, though it was not I, but the grace of God that is with me." (1 Corinthians 15:10). I have heard it said that "God doesn't call the qualified, he qualifies the called." I want you to know that it's God's grace that qualifies you to do what he calls you to do and to go where he calls you to go. You may be reading this book and feeling as if you are unqualified, but if God has called and chosen you, you must know that your past, your background, and your family history were not a factor in God's decision. It doesn't matter who you are or where you come from, God has plans for your life! However, those plans don't just happen, the fulfillment of those plans requires our participation.

You GO first

Abraham was chosen by God to do something that was out of the ordinary. No one else in his family had been called where he had been called to go and to do what he had been called to do. He was the first to follow and obey the one true God. He was the first of his family to make a faith move. By taking a step in the direction God had instructed him, he broke generational curses and opened the door for generational blessings for his lineage.

Have you ever felt like God was calling you to be the first in your family to do something very significant? Maybe not a geographical move, but the first to go get a college degree, start a business, or maybe the first to preach the gospel. Being the first of your family is hardly ever easy. Your decision may conflict with and break certain traditions that your family has held dear to their hearts for years.

I Must Keep Moving

Could you imagine the pressure Abraham must've been under when he had to break the news to his family that God was telling him to go? I have found this to be one of the greatest struggles most people face when God has told them to make a move.

There's no pressure like pressure from family. Often the pressure is so great because not everyone will understand the moves you must make for the sake of the future. They didn't hear what you heard, and they weren't there when you had an encounter with God that disturbed your comfort and provoked you to make moves. I have learned that pressure is a revealer. Pressure will reveal if you are truly committed to your "yes" to God and your decision to go!

Sometimes family members or friends who pressure us, hate to see us go because we are dear to them and most times they are comfortable with things just the way they are. Knowing this, helps us to not assume that the pressure from family members or peers means that they don't desire the best for us. People can desire the best for you, yet feel a certain way when your decisions affect the dynamics of the relationship you have with them.

I want you to know that you cannot afford to allow other people's feelings, words, doubts, misunderstandings, or criticism to make you question if you should really go. It's okay to care about our loved ones, but we are not obligated to consider their feelings when God is telling us to go. In fact, going may be more beneficial for them than you staying. Learn to embrace the honor and the pressure of going first. You were created to be a forerunner, a trendsetter, a trailblazer, a pioneer! Be the first! Even if you're not the first in your family to do something, be the first to do it on a level that's never been done before. Start your journey and stay committed to it! Go!

Going often means leaving something or people behind that you love. I have learned that destiny does not come on our terms. It will not just fall into your lap, it may require you to walk away, separate, and even disconnect from some things or people.

Going also means that there is a departure and an arrival. There's a departure from your current location and an arrival at your new destination. I don't think that it's an accident or by chance that the writer pens 3 specific things God asks Abram to depart from: "Go from your country, your people, and your father's household."

"GO from your country"

The word country in Hebrew means "territory, land." The territory in which Abram lived was called Ur of the Chaldees. This city was considered to be the center of moon worship. Based on what we know from Genesis 1, God created the moon. They worshipped creation rather than the creator. We weren't created to worship creation, we were created to worship the creator. God, who created the heavens and the earth created us for his glory. When I hear the word "territory," the first thing that comes to mind is "environment". When it comes to your purpose, your destiny, and your future, environments matter. Believe it or not, your choices, decisions, perspectives, and beliefs are influenced by the environments you place yourself in. The wrong environment can ruin great potential. It is like placing good seed in bad ground. A seed is full of potential to become more than what meets the eye. God promised to bless Abraham's seed, but he knew in order for the seed to reach its greatest potential, then he had to get it in the right ground or rather, environment. Sometimes God telling you to go isn't so much about you, but what you carry! God gives instructions for the sake of protecting your potential and fulfilling His eternal plan.

"GO from your people"

The KJV bible reads "Get from your kindred." Kindred means "family," or "relatives." One of the hardest things for most people to do is to move away from their families. If you're a big family person, this is probably the greatest struggle you may face when

GO!

you receive a word from God, a dream, or a vision that calls for you to change your geographical location. These aren't just mere associates, these are people whom we've grown up knowing and spending time with. Cousins who are our best friends, grandparents we make memories with, and even brothers and sisters we go on adventures and take trips with. These people are dear to us and matter to us. They have influenced and impacted our lives on some level. I can admit, that considering everything I have already mentioned, leaving can be a challenge.

The etymology of the word "relative" means "to refer," or "to relate." With family, we are related by blood, with friends we are related by our experiences or what we have in common. Abram wasn't just leaving family behind, but he was also leaving friends behind.

In March 2016, during my spring break in college, I planned a trip to Ormond Beach, FL to visit my spiritual parents at Calvary Christian Center. I was so excited that I could hardly contain myself. I had been so frustrated, disappointed, and confused by life. I was just two months away from getting my B.A. in English, and I had no idea what was next for me. A change of scenery is what I felt was just what I needed. Flying on the plane made all my issues seem as small as everything I saw on the ground beneath me.

The next morning, I went into the church offices with my spiritual father. We walked around and I met some incredible people. Some of the most amazing, spirit-filled, Jesus-loving people you will ever meet are on staff at Calvary Christian Center. I walked into the sanctuary and it was the biggest sanctuary I had ever been in, in my life. The stage, the screens, the lights, the chairs, the cameras, I was exposed to church on a level I had never seen before. The seats weren't filled, the lights weren't on, and there were no singers singing, no music in the background, but I felt something inside me leap and in a moment the Lord had given me an internal glimpse of my destiny. I didn't know all of what lay ahead, but I knew it would mean leaving family and some friends behind. I will discuss more about that later in this book.

"GO from your father's house"

I had an amazing father, and I thank God for him. My dad had driven trucks for as long as I have known him. Anything I would've needed, even to this day, he would've given me if he had it. My father was always a hard-working man. I can remember as a child when he would come home every night at 9. It seemed like he walked through the door at exactly 9 every weeknight. Regardless of what events may have taken place in his absence during the day, there

GO!

was always something about his presence that seemed to set the tone of the house.

I believe good fathers set the tone of the home through their presence, actions, their attitude, and the life lessons that they impart into us. We love them, we cherish them, we respect them because they are our fathers or father figures. When we are younger, we embrace almost everything they tell us without any question. We trust them, we trust that they won't lead us wrong or steer us in the wrong direction. For people who've grown up with a father in the home, who was active in their lives, a lot of their beliefs and perspectives on life have been instilled within them by their father. For most of us, we do the things that we do, because that's how our fathers taught us. My dad taught me when I was younger that if someone at school were to hit me, then I was supposed to hit them back. I remember the first time I tried that in elementary school, I got in a fight and very big trouble for it. What's my point? My dad loves me, and he wants me to protect myself, and he wants what is best for me. What he taught me, worked for the culture of our home, but it didn't work at the school. God telling Abraham to go from his father's house wasn't just to get him to leave a physical building, but it was also to get him to disconnect from a certain culture. With culture, there are certain belief systems, values, opinions, and behaviors that are not transferrable to other cultures.

I Must Keep Moving

Going isn't just departing from a geographical location, but it can also be departing from a certain way of thinking or believing that could hinder you from embracing all that God has for you.

The Blessing in Going

Just like it's God's will that you go, it's also his will to bless you as you go. As God spoke to Abram, he made several "I will" statements. Anytime God says, "I will," there's no question if something is his will or not. Sometimes the struggle isn't if God can, but believing God will. I want you to know that if God has made you a promise, it will come to pass. He's a God who cannot and will not lie. There are no empty promises with God, and neither is there idle talk with him. God doesn't waste words. If you've got a word from God, then you have the will of God. His will is revealed through his word. Remember, "Out of the abundance of the heart, the mouth speaks." Every word out of His mouth is truth, if God says that he will do something, he will do it.

GO!

"Unto a land that I will show you"

There are things that God wants to show you, but you will not see them until you're willing to make the decision to go. I wonder what you haven't seen yet because you haven't gone yet. He says, "unto a land," meaning "territory." There's territory that God has for you! It's one thing to claim it, but it's another to possess it. God asks Abram to leave one territory because he wants to give him another. Nothing God asks you to leave behind compares to what he has for you up ahead.

"I will make of you a great nation."

This was God's promise to Abram that he would be the first of an entirely new nation of people. You will be amazed at all that you will become as a result of your obedience to the Lord.

"I will bless you."

Being blessed is God's idea. God desires that you are blessed because he has the best in mind for you. Is that what you desire for yourself, your family, your ministry, or your business, how about your city or your nation? Notice that this blessing wasn't attached to his staying, but his going. There are blessings with your name on them that are attached to your decision to go.

The word *bless* comes from the Hebrew word *barak,* which means "to favor," to make successful and prosperous. God wants to favor you, and he wants your life to be prosperous and successful. Say this with me, "I am blessed because God wants me blessed. I am favored because God has favored me. My life will be prosperous and successful in Jesus' name!"

"I will make your name great."

For many years I've read that statement and thought that it meant that God wanted to make Abram popular. In fact, that's how I've heard it preached growing up in certain church cultures, that God wants to make us popular or famous.

I have learned that anyone who has identity issues, insecurities, or low self-esteem desires to be popular. From the time I began middle school until my sophomore year of high school, I was constantly picked on by some of my peers. I hated myself because certain people around me bullied me and didn't value me the way I wanted. I watched how they treated the "popular" people, and what made them so popular. Popularity then was based on how much money your parents made, what neighborhood you lived in, the clothes and shoes you

GO!

wore, and even your looks. Most adults today still struggle with how they perceive themselves because of how they were perceived in school when they were younger. I am convinced that a lot of the insecurities that we see in a lot of adults, whether young or old, have affected the way that they interpret the bible. Because of these insecurities, ministry becomes about selfish ambition and the applause of man. Insecurity has the ability to corrupt your desires and produce the wrong motives for why you do what you do. John 12:43 says, "For they loved the praise of men more than the praise of God." John was referring here to the Pharisees. The word praise in this verse comes from the Greek word "doxa" which means, "opinion, honor, glory." When I read this, it was a game-changer for me. This tells me that people have an opinion of me, and God has an opinion of me. Before we are created, we were first an idea in the mind of God. Before people could see you and interact with you long enough to even form an opinion about you, God had an opinion of you first. The reason the Pharisees loved the praise of men more than the praise of God was because it brought them instant gratification. The benefits were popularity and applause, but not a great name. I don't know about you, but I don't just want to be popular, but I want a great name. Great names are often tied to great character and accomplishments that served humanity in a great capacity. Never confuse a great name with a popular name. Although a great name by default is a popular name, a popular name isn't always a great name. God making your name great means that he makes you credible, influential, and honorable.

"You shall be a blessing"

Whenever God blesses you, he doesn't just bless you for you, but he also blesses you to be a blessing to someone else. Like many other kids, when I was younger, I wanted to be a millionaire, and I still do, but my reasons have changed. When you're a kid, there are two significant reasons why you probably desire to be rich: to buy whatever you want or to rescue your family from poverty. When God blesses us or rather favors us, he favors us to also extend favor to others. I have learned that God doesn't give us favor to flaunt, he gives us favor for fulfillment. It is within our human will to open a door of favor to someone who needs it for their purpose, destiny, dreams, and goals. You could be the opportunity that someone is waiting on! Favoring them with your knowledge, your resources, or even your connections could shift everything in their lives.

Being a blessing isn't just giving people material things, but also giving them spiritual things. Blessing others can be as simple as sharing your wisdom that helps someone else to prosper or succeed. The blessing is never just about you, but it is often about what's bigger and beyond you.

"I will bless them that bless you, and curse them that curse you."

Curse here is the opposite of "bless". Curse here comes from the Hebrew word "qalal" which means "to despise," or dishonor. He promised Abram that he would bring destruction upon those who opposed, dishonored, and despised him to the point of persecuting him.

"In you shall all the families of the earth be blessed."

Here's why you have to go because there's a generational blessing that God is waiting and ready to release on your life. According to Galatians 3:8, the blessing that God was referring to, was the justification of humanity through the shed blood of Jesus Christ. Because of Abraham's faith and obedience, people of every nation are able to come to the Lord and be saved. One "yes" to God today can affect generations. Making a decision to go isn't just for you, but also for people in every nation around the world. Abraham was carrying seed that God wanted to bless. Remember, great potential lies within a seed. God wants to bless what's in you so

I Must Keep Moving

that it blesses the world around you! He wants to favor you and make you prosperous, and successful. God has great plans for you and what you carry, it's bigger than what you could ever imagine. It's time to go!

PRINCIPLES OF PERSEVERANCE

1. God's plans for your life require your participation.

2. Pressure reveals if you're truly committed to God and your decision to go.

3. Destiny doesn't come on your terms, it may require you to walk away, separate, and disconnect from certain people or things.

4. God gives instructions for the sake of protecting your potential and fulfilling his eternal plans.

5. Your faith and obedience can break generational curses and open the door for generational blessings.

Chapter 2
Departure

"So Abram departed, AS the Lord had spoken unto him."

-Genesis 12:4

God had spoken to Abram to make a move, at the end of the day the decision was up to him to move. "God moves" are hardly ever easy, but necessary. When you're about to depart, whether it's geographically, spiritually, mentally, or emotionally, expect God to take you through a process.

It was a cold brisk Friday morning, March 2010, a day I'll never forget. I awakened to knots in my stomach. Why? Because it was the first day I had ever flown on an airplane. I was so afraid and nervous because I didn't know what to expect. I can remember running around frantically that morning

I Must Keep Moving

trying to figure out at the last minute what I wanted to bring. I googled "items that are allowed on an airplane." I realized that I had packed things in my bag that weren't allowed to be taken on the plane with me. Nothing I had packed was travel size. I kept thinking to myself, "I don't want to get kicked off the plane." "I don't want to be the headline on every major news station as the guy labeled a terrorist." "What do I do," is what I thought to myself. Good thing my mom was kind enough to allow me to do some last-minute shopping.

    We pull up to RDU and this place is huge. I get out of the car grab my bags, kiss my mom goodbye, and walk in. As soon as I walk in, I go right into panic mode because I have no idea where to go or even who to talk to. I ask a gentleman in an airline uniform, who's walking towards me if he could help me to figure out what to do first. He points me to a machine where I print out my ticket and a line where I check in my bags. I print out my ticket and I read where it says "departure", "seat," and "gate." I realized that every detail was important; from the time of our departure to the seat I paid for to the gate we were leaving from. I proceeded to check my bags in and the woman behind the counter asked if I had a carry-on bag. Me being nervous, I paid for both bags to go under the plane. I carried nothing on the plane but my iPhone, my iPad, and my headphones.

Departure

As I reflect on this moment in my experience, I can't help but find a connection to life. With that being said, as you have made up your mind that you're going to go as God has spoken, might I ask, "What's in your carry-on bag?"

After the tragedy of 911, airport security has increased, and airlines have become picky about the items that are allowed on airplane. Why? Because someone may bring an item on the plane that has the potential to be a weapon and could harm the lives of others. What do you have in your carry-on bag that has the potential to harm others or even yourself? Is it bitterness, unforgiveness, jealousy? How about anger issues, past hurt, or pain? What have you planned to carry with you on your journey to where God is calling you? If you're trying to carry something on your journey that has the potential to hurt or harm other people, you may ruin great relationships that are meant to be an asset to your destiny and purpose. I have found that purpose cannot be fulfilled alone. People need people in order to be successful at purpose. How healthy are your relationships, friendships, and connections? You have too big of a dream, great potential, and an incredible calling to carry things with you that will only hinder the success of your journey.

Shoes off!

After I checked in my bags, the woman at the counter pointed me to the next part of the departure process, airport security. Again, I'm so nervous, because I have no idea what to expect. As I approach, there's a long line, I think to myself "This will take forever." After about 15 minutes, I am the 5th person and all I hear is, "All electronic devices, carry-on bags, items in your pockets, or anything metal should be placed in a bin." So as I'm placing my items in a bin, a gentleman walks up and yells at us "HEY! ALL SHOES SHOULD BE PLACED IN A BIN. Immediately my eyes are really big, and I start to sweat from being nervous because I know in the back of my mind that I have a hole in my sock. I take off my shoes and it literally felt in that moment that the whole world stopped and looked down at my socks. I was so embarrassed. Then I began to look around and I saw people confused as to whether we leave our socks on or take them off. Like myself, some left their socks on, others took them off. I began to notice that there were people who were more nervous and embarrassed than I was. Why? Some people are self-conscious about their feet. We felt so vulnerable because of what we had to take off. People were exposing a part of their body or like me, a hole they didn't want anyone to see. We then step

Departure

into a full body scanner, receive a pat-down, and our bins are placed on a conveyor belt for screening. To someone who's never flown before, this process may sound invasive or unnecessary, however, the process was only for our safety as well as the safety of others.

In December 2001, a man named Richard Reid, also known as the shoe bomber tried to ignite explosives hidden in shoes. Reid never succeeded at fulfilling his agenda. Thank God no lives were harmed or lost.

God wants you to make it safely to your destination. When I think about having to take my shoes off, I can't help but think about when God told Moses to take off his shoes because the place he stood on was holy ground. For years, I had wondered why God commanded Moses to do that, but it wasn't until my airport experience that I realized that God wanted Moses to be vulnerable and to expose a certain part of himself in his presence. What made the ground holy was God's presence. God is holy. Whenever we are in his presence, he desires us to humble ourselves enough to be vulnerable and expose parts of ourselves we probably don't want anyone else to see. It's all a part of the process. I have learned that nothing reveals pride like being asked to remove something that exposes a flaw, a weakness, or insecurity. **God would rather you kill your pride before your pride kills you.** Proverbs 16:18 says,

I Must Keep Moving

"Pride goes before destruction." If you care more about preserving an image rather than your safety, then you have placed yourself on a platform for destruction.

Pride is like the explosives Reid tried to hide in his shoes. Pride doesn't just destroy those around you, but it is a setup for self-destruction. After doing research on Airport security, I have found that almost all of their processes and procedures are the result of tragic events or safety hazards in the past. Don't despise the process God takes you through before you depart. Remember, his intentions are pure towards you, he wants what's best for you. He's looking out for your safety, as well as the safety of others.

Finally, after the security process, I proceeded to find the airline I was flying on and the gate my plane was leaving from. In any airport, there are TVs displaying the gates, and departure and arrival times of all flights. Because it was my first time flying, I saw something on the screens that puzzled me. Within the column entitled status, I noticed that some of the flights didn't have a time, instead it said *delayed*. In an airport, you will learn very quickly that when flights are delayed, people become very unhappy. People have very important business meetings, job opportunities, ministry assignments, or major events that they must be on time for. When flights are

Departure

delayed, people are frustrated, and angry, and often take out their frustrations on the airline workers. Unless you're someone who doesn't value time, people typically do not like to be late. Delays are frustrating to people who value their time.

This entire scenario is interesting because there is a connection that we find in the story of Abraham. Abraham's father's name was Terah. His name in Hebrew means "station". It denotes the idea of stopping or being at a "standstill." Have you ever been connected to someone whose life is at a standstill? They've settled for living, paycheck to paycheck, having a relationship on one level when they deserve better, settled with just getting by and the status quo. The reality is that some of the people that are this way are our loved ones. Beloved, I want to know that as much as you love and care about a family member or friend, you are not obligated to commit your life to people who have chosen to stop at one level in life and have chosen to go no further.

This is even more interesting because Terah also means "delay", it denotes the idea of wandering. There's nothing worse than being connected to a wanderer or being led by a wanderer. People who wander have no clarity of mind and purpose, they are unstable and just winging it through life with no sense of direction. I've seen likable people with huge personalities who have very persuasive voices, they rally people around them and make them believe that they are headed somewhere, when in reality these likable people had no vision. Nothing is more frustrating than being persuaded to follow someone who has no sense of direction.

Wandering leaders create wandering followers. Jesus says, "If the blind leads the blind, both fall into a ditch." Blindness has to do with vision. Leadership with no vision is what I call ditch leadership. Ditch leadership is all talk and hype that leads people into a pit of delay. When people are led into a pit of delay, they become frustrated about things they shout about and hope for, yet they never see. When you're in a pit of delay, you see very little to no progress or movement. It's time for you to disconnect from wanderers and people who are at a standstill. Life is too precious, and your purpose is too great to be delayed. Make up your mind that there will be no more delays in your destiny. God has big plans and many blessings that are awaiting your arrival.

When I saw that my flight would be leaving on time, that gave me such a feeling of relief. Airlines encourage people to arrive at least an hour before their flight leaves so that they don't miss their flight. With God, timing is everything. He gives us a window of time to make a move that is significant and is the perfect setup for our destiny and purpose.

Departure

Before boarding a plane, you are required to show your boarding pass to an airline worker so that he or she may scan it. On the boarding pass it tells you a seat that is assigned to you. The seat that is assigned to you is the seat you paid for. You cannot take the seat without paying the cost. I want you to know that destiny does not come without a cost. Everything that you may have lost or that God has told you to sacrifice and walk away from, for your destiny, and the process God has taken you through, was all about getting you to your seat, or rather your position. God will take you through a process just to get you in position. Remember, that's what it means to be "On your Mark", to get in position! God gets you in a position to begin! At some point, you must GO, you must depart, you must leave the line and begin the race he has set before you! We don't get on the mark to stay on the mark, we get on the mark with the intention to begin. Are you ready to begin your God-ordained journey? Let's go!

PRINCIPLES OF PERSEVERANCE

1. Whenever you make God moves, he will take you through a process.

2. You need people in order to be successful at your purpose.

3. God would rather you kill your pride before your pride kills you.

4. God takes you through a process to get you in a position to depart and arrive at a destination.

5. Enjoy the journey!

Chapter 3
Unexpected Circumstances

"And there was a famine in the land: and Abram went down into Egypt to sojourn there; for the famine was grievous in the land."

-Genesis 12:10

When God first spoke to me about moving to Florida, I was overwhelmed with joy as tears ran down my face. I was excited about all that he showed me, and everything he'd promised me in that moment. After I flew back home, I shared with my family and friends that God was calling me to make a move. It wasn't easy to share this news with some of them, but it was necessary. As I was sharing it with one of my brothers, he asked me if I already had my own place. Then it hit me, I had no idea where I was going to live and how I was going pay for furniture. Finding a place to live hadn't crossed my mind, so I had no idea where I would be staying. I began to panic internally, and thoughts of doubt began to consume my mind. I was telling everybody that I was leaving and that God had spoken to me, yet I didn't know where I was going to live. To be honest, I felt like a fool, and in some moments, like a liar. I thought to myself "What if I never get enough money to move," "What if I never find a place to live," "Everybody's going to think that I'm a liar," "What if I didn't hear God right," "what if that was just my emotions from the excitement of being in Florida at Calvary?"

Because I didn't have the provision, I began to question the promise. Have you ever questioned a promise from God because you didn't have what you knew you needed when you thought you needed it? I was excited about the move, but worried about the resources I needed to make the move and sustain myself. Thankfully, after a conversation with my spiritual parents, they offered to allow me to stay with them long enough to save up and find an apartment. Today, I am eternally grateful for them.

Whenever God speaks to us about something he's going to do in our lives, we have a certain expectation or picture in our minds of how things will play out. The more you walk with God, you learn that rarely does he cause things to play out

Unexpected Circumstances!

according to our current level of faith. I've learned through the word and my experiences that God uses the unexpected to grow our faith.

After several weeks of settling in, I knew it was time to search for an apartment. My brother was getting married in a couple of months, so we both went apartment hunting. After a couple of days, he and his wife got approved for an apartment. He told me the price range and all that was required, to see if I would get approved at the same place. I applied, showed my check stubs, they ran my credit, and I was denied. I immediately became discouraged, but I didn't stop there. I applied at the apartment complex next door. I went through the same process, only to find out that I wasn't approved once again. At that point, I went online and found 8 more potential living options. I applied and drove to each one of them only to find out that I either made too much money or not enough. I was very discouraged, disappointed, frustrated, and even sometimes confused. I had a word from God to make a move, so I expected everything to fall into place. When things didn't go as I had expected, I started to think to myself, "Well, maybe this isn't where God wants me to be; maybe he just wanted to expose me to it and send me back." I can remember my spiritual parents and my spiritual brothers encouraging me and telling me that God was going to provide. Honestly, it was difficult for me to embrace because I was faced with the reality of my situation, and the enemy played in my mind.

One particular day I applied for an apartment, except this time I had my dad cosign. The next day I found out that I didn't get approved for the apartment. I was very upset and frustrated. I remember going back to my brother's apartment that night very disappointed. The next day, I went into my office, and when I walked in, I sensed in my spirit a strong unction to pray. It was a fight to pray because of how I felt, my emotions were all over the place. So I started by finding things to thank God for. The more thankful I became and the more I praised God, I could feel the heaviness and disappointment begin to lift off of me. Isaiah 61:3 says that we have the garment of praise for the spirit of heaviness. Before I knew it, I started to declare the word of God over my life. I didn't just declare his written word, but I declared his spoken concerning my life. I'm not sure exactly how to put it into words, but the more I prayed, decreed, and declared, I could sense breakthrough in the spirit. I realized in that moment that I don't pray to feel better, I pray until my faith gets stronger. I did that for an entire week at least 5 times a day.

Not only was my faith stronger, but there was a persistence that developed in me. I searched and searched for more apartment options until finally I came across something and I remember telling God,

Unexpected Circumstances!

"Lord, this is my last option. This one is on you." I prayed and declared his word over my life once again, then I called the apartment office. When I got on the phone, I asked the woman about the 1-bedroom apartment, and I told her my situation. She replied, "Mr. McCray, we're running a special, if you get approved for the apartment on Thursday, are you able to move in on Friday?" I replied, "Absolutely!" On Thursday, when I walked into the office and sat down, the manager walked up to me, I handed her all my information, and she whispered to me that the girl who was sitting across the room was applying for the same apartment. She told me that whoever gets approved for it first, gets the apartment. When the woman turned to walk away, I jumped up, walked into the bathroom, and began to pray as I shut the door behind me. I prayed, "Lord, if this girl needs this apartment more than I do, then let her get it, because I know that you have something else for me." I walked out of the bathroom, the girl was gone, and the manager walked up to me and said, Mr. McCray, you have been approved for the apartment, would you like to take a tour of it?" I remember going, "Really?" Thank God, and of course I would!" As soon as I stepped into the apartment, a peace came over me, and I began to thank God for providing just what I needed. I told my spiritual parents, and my spiritual brothers what God had done, they were all excited and rejoiced with me. I moved in the next day, but before I started to move in my clothes, I stopped by the office to sign the lease and make my first payment. While I was there, I found out that the complex had recently gone under new management for only 2 weeks, and the special they had available was the first month's rent for free. What really shocked me was that the last day of the special was on the day that I moved in! As soon as I finished the process and received the keys, I walked into the apartment and began to pray over it, thank God for it, and sing praises unto him. How faithful is our God?

None of what I went through was expected. I didn't expect things to play out the way that they did. I didn't expect to encounter the circumstances I had faced. Could you imagine making a God move and encountering unexpected circumstances? Abram made a God move and encountered unexpected circumstances, in fact, he walked right into a famine. The decisions you make during unexpected circumstances are crucial to your future.

Abram is widely criticized by theologians and preachers for his actions in Egypt. He lied and said that his wife was his sister. Pharaoh wanted to take her as his wife until God made it known that he would suffer consequences. Believe it or not, the decisions that we make during unexpected circumstances can affect those around us. Abram was willing to lie just to protect himself, and his wife.

Unexpected Circumstances!

I'm not attempting to justify his actions, but looking at the situation from his perspective, he was a husband and a man who had great possessions along with servants, and his nephew Lot. Abram made a decision that he felt was best for himself, his family, and his things. Abram's decision was made out of fear for his life and his wife's. Fear will make you tell a lie just for the sake of survival and I've seen this many times. I've seen people who say that they believe and trust that God will provide for them, but when they are faced with unexpected circumstances, they are willing to lie and cheat the system just to get their needs met. You don't have to manipulate people into feeling sorry for you so that they give you what you need. I want you to know that you don't have to be fearful of whatever famine may be happening around you. You don't have to lie or cheat the system just to survive but trust that if God initiated a move or journey in your life, then he will provide everything you need along the way.

My story doesn't stop there. Now that I had an apartment, I needed furniture. I prayed earnestly every day, I tithed, sowed, and saved up as much money as I could. I window-shopped for furniture, developed a financial plan, and trusted God in the meantime. Before I left to go back to North Carolina for Thanksgiving, our Connections Pastors approached me and asked how things were going with the apartment and if I had furniture. I explained

I Must Keep Moving

to them my plan and that I had been looking around. They then whispered to each other, looked at me, and said "When you get back from your trip, come to our house and pick out which couch you want. We're moving and we're just trying to get rid of a few things. I asked, "for how much?" They replied, "oh nothing, just come pick out what you want." I stood there in awe. It may not seem like much to someone else, but during that season of my life, that meant a lot to me. When I returned from my trip, I went to their house to pick up the couch. We grabbed the couch, put it in the trailer, walked back in the house, and they said to me, "You can have this ottoman too, and we have a recliner you can have." At this point, I'm almost in tears. We carry the recliner and ottoman to the trailer, and as I'm walking back, they start bringing a lamp, two end tables, a bookshelf, and bar tools. The only thing I could think at that moment to say was "Really? Wow! Thank you so much!" They looked at me one more time and told me that they had two barely used king-size mattresses in the garage that I could have. I was so excited and thankful, that I could hardly find the words to say at that moment. I realized that I had everything I needed and the whole drive back to my apartment, I began to thank God and praise him for his faithfulness.

Unexpected Circumstances!

Say what you hear

"God has the best in mind for me!" This is what you must continue to tell yourself whenever you're faced with unexpected circumstances.

Romans 10:17 says, "So then, faith comes by hearing, hearing by the word of God." It's so easy to become moved by what we see, but "we walk by faith, not by sight." If God speaks something, remember, he's a God that cannot and will not lie! I have learned that the more I declare to myself what God has promised, my faith is stirred and sustained, and it empowers me to endure through unexpected circumstances. Whenever God speaks, he speaks with intention. There is no idle talk with God. He speaks on purpose for a purpose. When God speaks and we receive his word, it becomes an impartation. Faith is an impartation, and it is God's persuasion. How persuaded are you of what he said about you, your career, your family, your ministry, and your future? We can either be swayed by our circumstances or be persuaded by God's word. Faith is heaven's perspective on what we see. Faith is living by the reality of heaven while living on earth. The culture of God's kingdom is a faith culture.

Throughout this book, I will reiterate certain faith principles because it is my earnest desire that

I Must Keep Moving

you get them in your spirit so that you can persevere to your expected end!

Unexpected Circumstances!

PRINCIPLES OF PERSEVERANCE

1. God will use the unexpected as an opportunity to grow your faith.

2. Don't pray just to feel better, pray until your faith gets stronger.

3. The decisions you make during unexpected circumstances are crucial to your future and could affect the people around you.

4. You don't have to lie, cheat, and manipulate a system just to get your needs met. If God initiates the move, he will provide everything you need along the way.

5. Faith is stirred and sustained when you declare to yourself what God has spoken.

Chapter 4
You've got a lot to get rid of

In order to truly persevere on your journey, at some point it requires you to assess your surroundings to see who's really with you and who's just tagging along.

Abram's nephew Lot tagged along with him on his journey. I believe that Abram tolerated Lot because he was family. Abram probably assumed that because he was family, there was no need to worry about any potential harm that could be done. This, my friend, is far from the truth. There is a danger in tolerating certain connections on your journey. There will always be people who desire to go with you on your journey for the ride, but they can't handle where God is taking you. Their worldview, belief system, and opinions may conflict with yours.

Remember, God told Abram to leave his kindred. Lot was someone Abram could relate to as far as the family's culture, values, and belief system. Lot would serve to Abram as not only a reminder of where he had come from but also the residue of what he had to leave behind. There was a certain way of thinking and believing that God wanted Abram to depart from. Don't get me wrong, Lot wasn't a bad person, he just carried the culture of what Abram was trying to depart from.

Have you ever been connected to someone who only reminds you of your past or where you've come from? Who you used to be? What you used to do? What do they think you should or can't do? These are also the voices that say things like "I remember when you used to..., or you've always been that way, or "why would you do that? You know no one in our family does that. Don't break the family tradition, pass on the legacy, we've come from a long line of doctors. Why would you want to be a lawyer?" Maybe they're friends who say things like, "Oh no, don't leave! Who am I going to talk to now? Who will party with me on the weekend? Are you sure that's what you want? To do that? You know they don't make a lot of money in that career field, right? Why would you want to move to Texas? It's so hot, it's a huge place, plus they have rattlesnakes!"

You've got a lot to get rid of!

See, some people may not wholeheartedly agree with the direction God is taking you, but they will try to ride your coat tail long enough to receive some of the benefits from your journey.

Lot physically tagged along with Abram on his journey, but that's not the only way someone can tag along. Tagging along could mean a family member or friend who constantly calls you, texts you, facetimes you enough to stay a part of your journey regardless of the decision you've made to go a different direction in life. These same people who tag along give you no godly advice when you're about to make a decision that could potentially ruin what God wants to do in your life. Like Lot, they don't encourage you to pray to God when you're faced with unexpected circumstances, they just follow you wherever you go with no true commitment to your journey. You need connections that are an asset to your journey. Here's how you know you may be connected to a tag-along!

"Tag alongs" are:
1. Silent when you're not thinking straight.
2. Around, but not all in.
3. People who bring their junk, yet they contribute nothing to your journey.

I Must Keep Moving

Back to the altar

"Then Abram went up out Egypt, he and his wife and all that he had, and Lot with him, to the South. Abram was very rich in livestock, in silver, and in gold. And he went on his journey from the South as far as Bethel, to the place where his tent had been at the beginning, between Bethel and Ai, to the place of the altar which he had made there at first. And there Abram called on the name of the Lord."
-**Genesis 12:1-4**

Abram's decision to go down to Egypt and to lie to Pharaoh wasn't a wise or godly one, but the Lord's mercy helped him out of a bad situation. If you're going to persevere on your journey to what God promised, then you're going to need his mercy. David states that the Lord's mercies are new every morning, they are from everlasting to everlasting. In Psalm 23, David says: "goodness and mercy shall follow me all the days of my life." I'll never forget when the Lord gave me the revelation that goodness and mercy follow me to keep my past from catching up with me. I want you to know that goodness and mercy are taking care of what's behind you. Fear may have pushed you to make a decision that has stirred up trouble, but God has a way of getting you up and out. You may have made some mistakes, fallen into sin, or lost your way, but I want you to know that by God's grace and mercy, you can get up, get out, and

You've got a lot to get rid of!

move on. Your past can't get a grip and hold you when you've got goodness and mercy following you!

Because of the magnitude of the situation, Pharaoh demanded that Abram and his family be removed from the city. Abram and his family were rejected from Egypt. They were rejected from a source they had turned to for help in their time of worry, because of a famine. Rejection is God's protection, redirection, and preservation. Sometimes when life happens in between what God promised and the fulfillment of what he promised, we can make decisions that have the ability to temporarily knock us off course. Often those decisions are on the basis of our understanding. I have learned that God will allow rejection just to put us back on course. Regardless of the delays, setbacks, or trouble we may face, the promises of God are still yes and amen! God will do whatever it takes to get you to the place of possessing what he promised. When God gets you up and out, thank him for his faithfulness, let the past be the past, and keep it moving.

After Abram departs from Egypt, he doesn't just go anywhere, he goes back to the altar. The altar is a place of sacrifice, it is a place of worship. He doesn't see the famine and decides to run back to Haran or back to who he used to be, he goes back to an altar. You can't afford to go back to who you used to be, what you used to do, and in some cases, where you used to go. Your destiny is too great! God has made you some incredible promises with your name on them, and he's eager to see you possess all that he has for you.

Abram doesn't stand around and condemn himself for his choices nor does he complain about the rejection, instead, he goes back to worship. That's the power of God's goodness and mercy, it promotes worship.

I find it interesting that in the Old Testament, an altar was the place of worship. There was always an animal that was sacrificed on the altar. Even though we don't sacrifice animals anymore to worship God, but worship him in spirit and truth, when we worship, something still gets sacrificed. When we worship, things like pride, hidden agendas, unforgiveness, bitterness, fear, worry, frustration, anxiety, and many other things are sacrificed.

What's even more interesting is where the bible says that the altar is located; between Hai and Bethel. Hai in Hebrew means "ruins" or "heap"; Bethel means "house of God." Ruins are the remains of a city, a building, etc., that has been destroyed and is in a state of decay. Have you ever had to worship between ruins and God's voice? I have found that some of the most powerful worship is done in the middle when life on one end displays destruction, but you're having God encounters on the other. One part of your life seems like it's in ruins, the marriage, the job, your family, but you're having radical encounters in the house of the Lord. A miracle in the temple, but a mess at home.

Where Abram built the altar is also symbolic of the distinction between his old life and the new. The old life of sin is a life of decay and destruction, the new life is lived in the presence of God. What separated the old life from the new is who he worshipped. A life of worship unto the Lord draws the line between good and evil, right and wrong, holy and unholy, love and hate.

Hosea 4:1 mentions that there was no knowledge of God in the land. Where there is no knowledge of God, a life of decay and destruction is inevitable. Knowledge of God isn't mere head knowledge, but intimate knowledge. Satan is perfectly fine with you having a general head knowledge of God, but he's not okay with you knowing God's heart. When you know God's heart, not only do you know the plans that he has for you, but you also know his intentions. Worshippers trust God because they know his heart (intentions). God's intentions toward you are pure and good. It would have been easy for Abram to assume that God didn't want what was best for him, all because of a famine he had experienced that God didn't tell him about. When you are a worshipper you learn to trust God when what's happening around you seems like it's working against what he wants to do in you and through you. Whatever you do, don't lose your worship, you may lose some money, friends, jobs, or even family, but never lose your worship. Your worship is your strength, it is the power to endure.

It's Too Crowded

The unwanted conflict and frustration that affects your ability to persevere could be an indication that you have a "lot" to get rid of.

"Lot also, who went with Abram, had flocks and herds and tents. Now the land was not able to support them, that they might dwell together, for their possessions were so great that they could not dwell together. And there was strife between the herdsmen of Abram's livestock and the herdsmen of Lot's livestock. The Canaanites and the Perizzites then dwelt in the land. So Abram said to Lot, 'Please let there be no strife between you and me, and between my herdsmen and your herdsmen; for we are brethren. Is not the whole land before you? Please separate from me. If you take the left, then I will go to the right; or, if you go to the right, then I will go to the left.' And Lot lifted his eyes and saw all the plain of Jordan, that it was well watered everywhere (before the Lord destroyed Sodom and Gomorrah) like the garden of the Lord, like the land of Egypt as you go toward Zoar. Then Lot chose for himself all the plain of Jordan, and Lot journeyed east.

You've got a lot to get rid of!

And they separated from each other."
-Genesis 13:5-11

Confronting connections

Abram and his family weren't broke, they were not poor, they didn't live in poverty, they were rich the bible says that they were very rich. They had so many possessions, but they weren't exempt from problems. Possessions don't exempt us from problems. Their problem was space. The land could not support them both. There was not enough room, not enough capacity to handle all that both of them carried. When people connect to you or commit to your life, they don't just bring themselves, but they also bring their stuff. You must ask yourself, is there enough room? There are places where God wants to take you that everyone can't go, not because they are bad people, but because there isn't enough room in the place God is taking you, for your stuff and theirs. Abram's tolerance of Lot and his possessions created unwanted conflict. Had he confronted Lot in the beginning, the entire situation could have been avoided. **When it comes to certain connections in your life, what you tolerate and don't confront in the beginning will later create unwanted conflict.** Have you ever made a God move and now you're arguing with family members or friends because of all that you have going on and all that they have going on seems to be conflicting? Conflicting views, perspectives, beliefs, schedules, etc. When life happens, you need the boldness to confront every connection that's causing conflict in your life.

Separation

I believe that one aspect of life that's highly valued amongst humanity is attachment. To some degree, we are all attached to something or certain people. For a child, it could be a teddy bear or caregiver, for teenagers maybe their cellphones, for adults it could be a car or spouse. We are all attached to something. It is the presence of the thing we're attached to that brings us some type of comfort or benefit to our lives. For example: In high school, many of my peers gravitated to groups that gave them a sense of identity. When you're a teenager, you go through the process of trying to discover who you are and find where you fit. When you don't know your identity, you will tag along and attach yourself to people who make you feel important and give you a sense of validation of who you are.

Hopefully, you get an idea of the high value that is placed on attachment. Considering this reality helps you gain a sense of understanding as to why separation can be difficult for most people. Separation can be very difficult, but it is necessary for your destiny and purpose.

You've got a lot to get rid of!

"Separation promotes and announces distinction."

My spiritual father always says, "With God, separation isn't separation, separation is sanctification." Sanctification isn't just about what God wants to separate you from, but also what he separates you for. What he calls you to, and has chosen you for, will often make you distinct from others.

Going separate ways

Abram's heart and perspective on the situation struck me. He says "Please let there be no strife between you and me, we are brethren. Is not the whole land before you? Please separate from me" (see Genesis 13:8). Abram valued and cherished the nature of their relationship. He acknowledged that they were "brethren," not enemies. Conflict isn't always a sign that a friend or brethren is an enemy. Conflict could be a sign that there's just not enough room. Notice what Abram does, he makes Lot aware that there's land all around them. When you have to make a difficult decision to separate from people you love, you must help them see that it doesn't just benefit you, but it benefits them as well. Regardless of how they respond, be confident that you've done your part in helping them to see it from a more positive perspective. Show them that God doesn't just have a place he wants to take you, but he has a place for them as well.

In my own experiences and observations, I have seen several responses to this type of situation: some people respond with immediate anger or sadness and never grasp how it benefits them, while for others it takes time to process then they accept it. You have no reason to feel guilty or like the "bad guy." Making a decision to separate doesn't make you a "bad guy" regardless of what someone says or their actions in response to your decision. It saddens me to see people become trapped, stuck, and settle because of the emotional response of other people. Today, free yourself from the emotional responses of people who don't want to understand why you must disconnect. Remember, it's for your benefit and theirs, even though they can't see it.

"We become imprisoned by people's emotions when we value their perspective and opinion of us that has been filtered through a heart that does not understand. "

If you are currently living in this reality, free yourself from this prison by choosing to value God's promises, your destiny, and your purpose more than the opinions of others. Sometimes love is expressed

You've got a lot to get rid of!

through making the hard decision to separate. What are you fearful of? If God be for you, who can be against you? David says, "The LORD is on my side; I will not fear: what can man do unto me?" (Psalm 118:6). Let your confidence and courage be found in the reality of who's on your side. If God is on your side, then no opinion carries enough weight to make him change his mind about you or his promises for you. No need to fear! This is not a battle you need to fight, "set yourself, stand still, and see the salvation of the Lord!

PRINCIPLES OF PERSEVERANCE

1. You need connections that are an asset to your journey.

2. God's goodness and mercy clean up your past so that you can get up and move on.

3. Rejection is God's protection, redirection, and preservation.

4. Never lose your worship!

5. The unwanted conflict and frustration, that affects your ability to persevere, could be an indication that you have a lot to get rid of.

6. What you tolerate and don't confront in the beginning could later create unwanted conflict.

7. Conflict isn't always a sign that a friend or brethren is an enemy, it could just be a sign that there's just not enough room.

8. Making a decision to separate doesn't make you a "bad guy," regardless of what someone says or actions in response to your decision.

Chapter 5
I Must Keep Moving

Moving with Identity

It is knowing who are, what, and where you're called to that keeps you from looking back and going back. Who are you? Who do people think you are? How we perceive ourselves and who we think we are determines how we manifest ourselves to the people around us. The people around us either see who we think we are, who we know we are, or who they want us to be.

God believes in us more than we believe in ourselves. Why? Because God knows more about us than we know about ourselves. God created us. He knows how he wired us and what he put on the inside of us. God knows what makes us happy, sad, frustrated, what turns us off, and what turns us on. Sometimes God's belief in us creates internal conflict. This conflict is often the result of our perception and other people's perception of ourselves in comparison to how God sees us. Could you imagine being Moses? Born as a Hebrew, growing up in the house of an Egypt ruler (Pharaoh), and to make things even worse, having a speech impediment. Moses' past circumstances and his condition were major contributions to how he perceived himself. Moses said to God, "Who am I, that I should go unto Pharaoh, and that I should bring forth the children of Israel out of Egypt?" Moses had to recognize something, that God didn't just see the potential of what he could do, God knew who he was. Have you ever been conflicted in your perception of yourself and God's perception of you? Moses' response was an indication that he had yet to perceive himself the way that God did. How do you perceive you? Do you have the proper perception of yourself? How you perceive yourself is vital to the success of your God-given purpose and assignments. Not everyone sees you the way God does, but you must become convinced enough within yourself that if no one else sees you the way that you see you, it doesn't affect your confidence in knowing who you are.

    Moses was uncertain that he had what it took to complete the assignment that God was calling him to fulfill. I want you to know today that anytime God calls you to do something, you never have to worry about trying to fulfill it on your own. Remember, God is with you, so you've got what it takes.

Level up

"For my thoughts are not your thoughts, neither are your ways my ways, saith the Lord. For as the heavens are higher than the earth, so are my ways higher than your ways, and my thoughts than your thoughts."
                                                            -Isaiah 55:8, 9

If God believes in us more than we believe in ourselves, and his ways and thoughts are above ours, then how do we begin to see and think of ourselves on his level? The answer is found in verse 7. God says: "Let the wicked forsake his way, and the unrighteous man his thoughts." The answer can be summed up in one word, *repent*. The Greek word for *repentance* is metanoia; which means: "to have a change of mind or to think differently." Because we are born into this world as sinners separated from God, our minds are accustomed to thinking a certain way apart from God and his word.

Before we come into Christ, there are many beliefs, ideologies, perspectives, and even our worldviews that have been influenced by the world around us. To repent means having a willingness to abandon any beliefs, perspectives, and ideas that contradict the nature of God and his word; and having a willingness to embrace new thoughts and ideas. It takes humility to repent. When you repent, you are giving up not only what you think you know, but what could be years of having a mindset that has been geared one way.

If we are to embrace God's ideas, then it is important to know that his ideas are communicated through his word. The word, "confess" by Greek definition means "to agree." Therefore, the way that God's thoughts become our reality, and the way we train our minds to think on his level is by confessing his word. When we speak the word of God, we come into agreement with his thoughts. Say what he says about you, and you will begin to perceive yourself the way he sees you.

Are you sure?

God understands that his silence about who you are could possibly lead to your demise. This is why I believe God's public affirmation of Jesus during his baptism was so crucial. God spoke over him and said, "This is my beloved son in whom I'm well pleased." What a beautiful moment! Do you know that God does the same thing for you when you come into Christ? He says, "This is my beloved son/daughter in whom I am well pleased." He loves you with the same love that he has towards his son.

Perseverance by faith

Ephesians 1:6 says, "he has made us accepted in the beloved." The word *beloved* in Greek and this context means that "the same love God has towards his son is the same love that he has towards those who are His." God's love and affirmation of who we are must be enough for us in order to successfully persevere in life, fulfill our purpose, and possess every promise that he has for us. Identity fuels perseverance.

After God's affirmation and the Holy Spirit descended upon Jesus like a dove, Mark 1:12 says," and the holy spirit drove him into the wilderness to be tempted of Satan. I love that Mark uses the word *drove*, because, when the Holy Spirit comes, he doesn't come to be the passenger, he comes to be the driver. He wants to lead you somewhere. Ask yourself, how much of my life have I allowed the Holy Spirit to lead lately? Jesus was led into an uncomfortable season of temptation. Why would the Holy Spirit lead him into an uncomfortable place? The Holy Spirit may lead you to places that are uncomfortable, but he will never lead you to places that are unnecessary. Whenever the holy spirit leads you somewhere, he's intentional about where he leads you. The uncomfortable season is working for you, it's not working against you. It may not feel good but it's working for your good.

When I made the move from North Carolina to Florida, I kept asking God, "Why is it so uncomfortable, yet rewarding?" God spoke to me and said, "Don't you remember? This is what you prayed for, you said 'Lord, whatever you do don't let me settle.'" The will of God may be uncomfortable, but it is rewarding. I want you to know that the discomfort you may be experiencing is to keep you from settling. It is designed to keep you from settling with the wrong relationships, and the wrong job, and ultimately, to keep you from settling with doing life on the wrong level. The uncomfortable and testing season is there to reveal to you any deficiencies or flaws you may have in your perception of who you are.

When Jesus was tempted in the wilderness, he was tempted on the basis of his identity. Satan wanted him to perform in order to prove who he was. I want you to know that you do not have to perform to prove to people who you are. You are who God says you are. Let the Father's affirmation of you be enough. Jesus came out of the wilderness in the power of the Spirit. This season of your life may be uncomfortable, and it may seem like you're being tested on every angle, but I want you to know that at the end of the season, you will come out with power.

The Custom

"*He went to Nazareth, where he had been brought up, and on the Sabbath day, he went into the synagogue,*

Perseverance by faith

as was his custom. He stood up to read, and the scroll of the prophet Isaiah was handed to him. Unrolling it, he found the place where it is written: 'The Spirit of the Lord is on me, because he has anointed me to proclaim good news to the poor. He has sent me to proclaim freedom for the prisoners and recovery of sight for the blind, to set the oppressed free, to proclaim the year of the Lord's favor.' Then he rolled up the scroll, gave it back to the attendant and sat down. The eyes of everyone in the synagogue were fastened on him. He began by saying to them, 'Today this scripture is fulfilled in your hearing.'"

-Luke 4:16-21

A custom can be defined as widely accepted habitual practices or a usual way of behaving. It was a Jewish custom to go into the synagogue to sit and listen to someone read a scripture. Jesus shows up to read, but he's not just there to read a scripture, he's there to make an announcement. Jesus shows up in a familiar place to make an announcement. When you've had an encounter with God there are some familiar places and familiar faces you'll come across and make an announcement that something has changed.

The Cause

Jesus stands, clears his throat, and says "The Spirit of the Lord is upon me because he has anointed me." Jesus made a bold statement, it wasn't made in arrogance, but confidence. Be confident in what you carry and the anointing that's on you. You don't have to apologize for what's on you. God set it up that way, embrace it. I have learned that confidence is mistaken as arrogance to the insecure. Do not cast away your confidence. Confidence in what you carry fuels your ability to persevere.

Do you know that the anointing never comes without a cause? Also, God will never make you your own cause. People who fight for a cause are usually willing to give their lives for it. Jesus promised the disciples that after the holy spirit had come upon them, they would receive power to be witnesses unto him. Anytime God brings a cause to your life it will always be bigger than you. Whenever God calls you to something, he will never call you to something that you can fulfill in your own strength, it will always be beyond you. If you become successful at something he calls you to, and you do it without him, then only you get the glory and he doesn't. I don't know about you, but I want God to get glory, honor, and praise for every goal that I obtain, and every accomplishment make. God is the source of true success and fulfillment.

The Call

Birthed out of every cause is a call. The word call comes from the Greek word *klésis* which means "to invite." Whenever God calls you, it is an invitation to what you were born for. The call is an invitation to your purpose. When the Holy Spirit came upon Jesus in the wilderness, he didn't just receive power, he received an invitation. I have received many wedding invitations. Written on the invite card there's often a memo that says respond RSVP. When Jesus stood up to read, he was responding "RSVP."

After Jesus reads, he shuts the book and sits down. Immediately they responded, "Is this not Jesus, the son of Joseph?" They had a hard time perceiving what was on him and who he was because they were so familiar with him. When people are too familiar with you, they often have a hard time recognizing what's on you. Remember, Jesus says "A prophet is not without honor except his own hometown. You must learn to honor the anointing on your own life. There are some people who will receive you and there are some people who will not receive you. Either way, you must learn to honor the anointing on your own life. Be confident in this, you may not be sent to everybody, but you're sent to somebody.

The Conflict

After Jesus responded, people were angry. This is where the conflict began. There was a clash between old ways and perspectives, versus a new thing. Whenever you answer a call wholeheartedly, there are some customs that no longer fit you, and opinions that no longer move you. There are some behaviors, habits, fellowships, and friendships that you forsake because of the call. Remember, the call of God doesn't just separate you from others, but it also separates you for a specific purpose. Jesus understood that he was rejected by the same people in his hometown because he no longer fit their customs. Even when people reject you and misunderstand you, you must tell yourself, "I must keep moving." Rejection can be difficult, especially when it comes from family and friends who are closest to us. However, it is the change of our perspective about rejection that gives us the fuel to persevere.

In spite of all Jesus faced, he kept moving. He kept moving in the reality of his identity and he kept moving in ministry. In times of discomfort, you must keep moving. In times of misunderstanding, you must keep moving. In times of dishonor, you must keep moving. In times of conflict, you must keep moving. Jesus understood that there was a world waiting for what he carried, waiting for him to give

Perseverance by faith

himself for them. Certainty of your identity, what you carry, and what you were created for is what you need to persevere in life.

I Must Keep Moving

PRINCIPLES OF PERSEVERANCE

1. Knowing your identity, as well as, what and where you're called to, keeps you from looking back and going back.

2. How you perceive yourself is vital to the success of your God-given assignments and purpose.

3. Repentance is having the willingness to forsake any beliefs, perspectives, and ideas that conflict with the nature of God and his word; and having a willingness to embrace his thoughts and ideas.

4. God's love and affirmation must be enough for us in order to successfully persevere in life, fulfill our purpose, and possess every promise that he has for us.

5. The Holy Spirit may lead you into places that are uncomfortable but never places that are unnecessary.

6. Changing your perspective about rejection gives you the fuel to persevere.

7. Learn to honor the anointing on your life and be confident in it.

8. Tell yourself, "I must keep moving!

Chapter 6
Perseverance by faith

There is no doubt in my mind that there is not a single person in this world who imagines a world without trouble. A world without issues, problems, crises, sickness, disease, struggle, difficulty, a life where everything is perfect. We all desire a life where all of our needs are met or a body that is in complete health. A life where there's peace, harmony, love, and no turmoil. Regardless of who we are, where we've come from, how much money we have in the bank, what career field we are in, or what family we were born into, if there's one thing that all of humanity can attest to is that no one is exempt from trouble on some level.

In John 16:33 Jesus says, "In this world you will have tribulation, but be of good cheer for I have overcome the world. I have told you this that in me you may have peace." Jesus tells his disciples that there will always be trouble in the world. Someone may read this and think that he's trying to get them to embrace a negative mindset, but this is far from Jesus' intention. Jesus' purpose for telling them that trouble will always exist was to try to create a balanced expectation for them. There are people who like to think that having no expectations prevents disappointment. In my humble opinion, it is a balanced expectation that decreases the chance of disappointment.

    Jesus wasn't trying to get his disciples to take on a negative mindset, he was trying to get them to embrace truth. Jesus says, "You shall know the truth and the truth shall make you free" (John 8:32). To resist truth is to resist freedom. You may ask yourself how can embracing the reality that trouble will always exist in this world grant freedom? Embracing this truth frees you from imbalanced expectations that lead to lifetime disappointment. When you expect life to eventually be perfect, to have perfect circumstances, the perfect job, the perfect career, the perfect family, the perfect ministry, the perfect city, the perfect nation, a perfect country, the perfect world, you have a hard time embracing that this will never be a world without trouble. Jesus told us trouble will always exist, but be of good cheer.

Perseverance by faith

The presence of trouble does not negate the presence of God. In Psalm 46:1 the writer states that God is a very present help in trouble. This is why it's important to develop your relationship with God so that you know his heart and you know his intentions towards you. One of the greatest revelations in life that you could have is the revelation of God's goodness, a revelation of his heart. Once you know God intimately then you no longer view him through the lens of how people treat you.

When you're going through a time of difficulty, loss sickness, disease, a struggle, people may walk out of your life, abandon you, and gossip about you, but God promises that he will never leave you nor for sake you. Know today, that trouble may be present, but God is not absent! If God does not immediately deliver you out of it, then know that he's in it with you.

If there's one thing that I believe that has marked me as an individual, it's my smile. I have people who say to me all the time, "You're always smiling, why are you always smiling? Every time I see you, you're smiling, why do you smile so much?" If you want to know the secret, here's the secret: The secret to my smile is my perspective. The same truth that Jesus spoke to his disciples, is the same truth that I have embraced in my own life.

I do not live a life of perfect circumstances. I do not live a life where all my ducks are in a row. I do not live a life that is trouble-free. Life happens to me just like it happens to anyone else. But I choose not to allow my circumstances to control my thinking and dictate the quality of life I live while on this earth. The Bible says "We walk by faith and not by sight" (2 Cor. 5:7). Faith is not the denial of our reality. Faith isn't living in a fantasy world. Faith is not psyching ourselves out and acting as if what we hear, see, touch, taste, and smell does not exist. Faith is not allowing what you see to determine how you respond to life. Faith is allowing God's written and spoken word to determine how you respond to what you see. You will respond to life either according to what God says or what you see.

God speaks in many different ways. It is of great benefit to your life to be able to discern when God is speaking and the means through which he speaks. God spoke to Abram in a vision. God says to him, "I am your shield, your exceedingly great reward." The word *shield* there in Hebrew means "protector" or "one who protects citizens with force. Because you are a citizen of his kingdom, he has bound himself by his own law to protect your well-being.

God speaks through visions. Have you ever had God make you precious promises, but the circumstances around you seem like they aren't the proper conditions that can yield what God promised you? Abraham and Sarah had all these promises

Perseverance by faith

from God but had to deal with the reality of Sarah's barrenness. When we are moved by what we see we start to question what God said.

I want to encourage you that regardless of what you see, it does not negate the promises of God. God's promises to your life and the lives of those whom you are connected to, are forever yes and amen. I find it amazing that God already knew how old Abraham and Sarah were, yet he still made them promises. God's promises to your life are never on the basis of the circumstances that surround you, they are on the basis of his will, purpose, and intent for your life. God wants what's best for you and it's time for you to embrace that reality. Regardless of what happens to you, what you face, or how things may look now, know that God wants and desires nothing but the best for his children. People may betray you, you may lose a loved one, or you may have lost a house or even a job, but know today that God wants and desires what is best for you. God specializes in impossible situations. He specializes in chaos, trouble, and tragedy. When the angel Gabriel spoke to Mary, she was in a very similar situation as Sarah, he said to her, "With God, nothing shall be impossible with God all things are possible" (Matthew 19:26).

Hebrews 6:15 says in reference to Abraham, "And so, after he had patiently endured, he obtained the promise. Abraham received the promises of God with patience. I want you to know that your faith is meant to be tested. according to James 1:1, "the testing of your faith produces endurance" or should I say perseverance. Perseverance is simply the ability to remain under a challenge or trial while being unmoved from your purpose and devotion to God. The enemy knows that if he can move you, then he can cause you to forfeit what God promised you. Make up in your mind today that regardless of the circumstances that may surround you and the situations you may find yourself in, you will not allow anyone or anything to talk you out of what God promised you.

In 1 Timothy 6:12, Paul says to Timothy, "fight the good fight of faith." One thing I want you to know is that it's a good fight. It's a fight that is worth fighting. It is a fight that will benefit you and defeat what's fighting against you. Romans 10:17 says "Faith comes by hearing and hearing by the word of God." To fight the good fight of faith means to fight to maintain and hold on to the reality of what God said. Whether it's what he has spoken audibly or what he has spoken in his word. Abraham and Sarah had to fight the good fight of faith. Let me ask you, "Is there a fight in you?" Sometimes we lose at life because we are too passive, we let things just happen to us and we don't fight back. While I am aware that there are just some things that are beyond our control, we do not have to allow the things that we

Perseverance by faith

cannot control to determine the state of our minds and the state of our health, and our bodies. People are going to say things, people are going to do things, and Satan is going to do what he does which is lie, kill, steal, and destroy. He is the enemy of our lives. He is not a passive enemy, but he is an enemy that is active and proactive. You cannot be passive with an aggressive enemy, you've got to have a fight in you.

Make up in your mind today that you're going to fight back. Fight back with the word of God. Fight back with what God says. Sickness may be in your body, his word that says, "By his stripes, you were healed." They may come and repo your car or you may lose your home, but fight back with the word of God, knowing that he will supply all of your needs according to his riches in glory.

Remember when God spoke to Abraham in a vision and said to him "I am your shield and exceeding great reward"? What comforting words are these from our heavenly father, that in the face of trouble, he's our shield. When the enemy comes against us and we are surrounded by enemies who have come to destroy our lives, steal our passion, or cause us to forfeit our purpose and even our destiny, God himself is our protector. Abraham had begun to think that because of what he didn't have, the promises of God were negated in his life. God had made promises to Abraham and his seed. However, Abraham didn't have a child at the time. Abraham assumed that he knew who would be his heir. Sometimes we think we know the outcome of the situation because of, or on the basis of our own reasoning and logic.

    Instead of rebuking Abraham, God gave him a point of reference. "And He took him outside and said, 'Now look toward the heavens, and count the stars, if you are able to count them." And He said to him, "So shall your descendants" (Genesis 15:5). God's way of sustaining your faith is by giving you a point of reference to remind you of what he promised you. Every time Abraham walked outside and looked up at the stars, he would be reminded of what God promised him. Anytime he had become discouraged by what things looked like in the natural, he could just look up at the stars and be reminded of God's precious promises to him and his seed. God has amazing promises for you and for people that you are connected to! I want to encourage you, be not weary in well doing!

    "And he believed in the Lord and he counted it to him for righteousness" (see Genesis 15:6). The word righteousness in this context has two meanings. Righteousness in Hebrew means probity and piety. In the next chapter we will discuss it from the aspect of probity but let's look at it in terms of piety. Piety means devotion. Abraham's belief in the Lord and his promises was a sign of his devotion to God. When the conditions around you seem to be

Perseverance by faith

unfavorable to what God promised, what God looks for is your continued devotion to him. God is a God of covenant. Anytime God makes a statement that begins with "I will," he is establishing a covenant. Therefore, the second way that God helps sustain our faith is by renewal of his covenant.

Because of all that Abram was surrounded by, he began to have doubts about what God spoke to him. In the midst of his doubts, God renews his covenant with him. When we pray, praise, worship, or read the word of God we will experience moments where God renews his covenant with us. The renewal isn't just a refreshing of our memories, but a refreshing of our soul. David says, "As the deer pants for the water brooks so my soul longs for thee." It is in his presence that he removes corrupted thoughts of doubt and uncertainty and refreshes our souls with the reality of his promises and the covenant that he has made to us. This is why it is important to write down whatever God speaks to you. That way, when life happens, you are able to go back and remind yourself and refresh yourself with the reality of God's covenant in everything he promised you. Not only should you go back and read what he has promised and read his covenant, but you should declare it over your life out loud. Life is loud, but you must speak louder. Faith isn't just hearing the word of God but it's also speaking the word of God. Faith is vocal. Death and life are in the power of the tongue.

I Must Keep Moving

Living by faith isn't just believing God for something, it is also living in the reality of what God says about you. God changed Abram's name to Abraham. Abraham means father of many nations. Why would he change his name? God understands the importance of a name. Tied to every name is a history and a destiny. As long as he was called Abram he would be identified by his history, but as long as he was called Abraham he would be identified by his destiny. It is God's desire that we thank him for our history, but we identify ourselves according to our destiny. Your destiny is too great for you to be bound by your history. It becomes a bit easier to persevere when we get the right perception of ourselves and God. When we learn to see ourselves the way God sees us and identify ourselves the way that God does, when life happens, we live in the reality of knowing that we are more than conquerors through him who loves us! Persevere by faith!

PRINCIPLES OF PERSEVERANCE

1. Balanced expectations decrease the chance of disappointment.

2. To resist truth is to resist freedom, to embrace truth is to embrace freedom.

3. Know God intimately so that you aren't reduced to viewing him through how people treat you.

4. Faith is allowing God's written and spoken word to determine how you respond to what you see.

5. The circumstances around you don't negate the promises of God.

6. Perseverance is simply the ability to remain under a challenge or trial while being unmoved from your purpose and devotion to God.

7. You cannot be passive with an aggressive enemy, you must have some fight in you.

I Must Keep Moving

8. Write down what God speaks to you so that when life happens, there is way less confusion about what he said.

Chapter 7
Persevering with Integrity

"Then the LORD asked Satan, "Have you noticed my servant Job? He is the finest man in all the earth. He is blameless--a man of complete integrity. He fears God and stays away from evil. And he has maintained his integrity, even though you urged me to harm him without cause."

-Job 2:3

If there's one thing that I've learned from my spiritual father, it is that core values are important. Your core values are your standards that you refuse to compromise no matter what. I have a friend whose favorite quote is "Integrity is vital." If you were to go to his Facebook page or Twitter right now, you would find that quote at the end of every post he makes. He has written this quote at the end of every post almost every day since he started his Facebook page. The fact that he commits to writing this at the end of every post tells me that integrity is something that he highly values. If you are going to successfully persevere in life, another key component you'll need is integrity. The etymology of the word integrity is blamelessness, innocence, and purity. God desires for us to live blameless lives. When the Bible instructs us to live blameless lives, it isn't referring to moral perfection where we make no mistakes and have no flaws. To live a blameless life is to live a life of honesty, character, and innocence.

Job was a man who feared the Lord, he was considered a just man who was upright and perfect. Although he was a man who feared the Lord, he still experienced one of the most tragic seasons of his life. He experienced tragedy on a level that he'd never imagined he would face. He experienced life's circumstances to a degree that he felt like he didn't deserve. Most people ask the question, why do bad things happen to good people? In the context of the story, Job had done nothing wrong. In fact, he had done everything right. Job feared the Lord and loved the Lord so much that he was considered by God to prove to Satan this reality. Even Satan wondered if Job feared the Lord for no reason. Satan said to God "Put forth the thine hand now and touch all he has and he will curse you to your face." And the Lord said unto Satan, "Behold all that you have is that he

Persevering with Integrity

has is in your power." Satan could touch Job's stuff, but he could not touch Job's soul. Satan was after Job's reverence and love for God. **It is when tragedy strikes your life and circumstances arise that the condition of your heart is truly revealed.**

If there's anyone in the Bible who knows what it's like when life happens, it is certainly Job. Job lost everything that he had: his children, and possessions, and there was even an attack on his health. Could you imagine the pain, grief, sorrow, confusion, and pressure in the season of life Job was experiencing?

God wanted to prove to Satan that Job's life of devotion was not motivated by the things he possessed or the people who were in his life. What motivates you to do what you do for the Lord? Why do you serve the Lord? What motivates you to read your bible, and attend/serve at your local church? Do tragedy and circumstances affect your worship and praise? Take a moment to ask yourself these questions and allow God to reveal your heart to you. If you find that your heart isn't truly for the Lord out of pure reverence for him, this is the perfect opportunity to change the posture of your heart. David said, "Create in me a clean heart." The condition of your heart will always be reflected through your actions. When your heart is turned towards the Lord, there's no trial or circumstance that can determine your level of devotion to God. God doesn't bless us to motivate us to serve him, serving him is motivated by his love for us and our love for him.

Choose to worship

After receiving the bad news, Job arose, fell to the ground, and worshipped. When we receive bad news, a typical response is either sadness, anger, or confusion but after Job received bad news he chose to worship. When you don't understand, worship. When all hell is breaking loose in your life, worship. When you lose things that are most precious to you, things that you are attached to, when people walk out of your life, or even when it looks like you're losing to a terminal sickness, always choose the worship. Worship is reverencing God according to his worth. His worth isn't determined by what he does or doesn't do, his worth is determined by who he is.

Don't blame God

Never blame God for what the devil does. I have seen many people who have experienced the loss of a loved one, a tragic accident, the foreclosing of a home, the repossession of a car, or sickness in their body and they've blamed God. Nothing hinders your capacity to persevere like a poor understanding of God's sovereignty and his will. It is common among humanity to develop our own conclusions that give us a sense of comfort to help us cope with the tragedies that we experience. When something tragic happens in our lives or the lives of another individual, it is often or typically smoothed over by a blanket statement such as well this must be the will of God. The Bible says that there is a way that seems right to man but the end thereof is death and destruction. As long as you continue to blame God for what the devil does, then overtime your heart will grow hardened towards God and you will think that he's a God who does not want or desire the best for you, your family, your friends, your country, and the entire world.

Friends

"When Job's three friends, Eliphaz the Temanite, Bildad the Shuhite, and Zophar the Naamathite, heard about all the troubles that had come upon him, they set out from their homes and met together by agreement to go and sympathize with him and comfort him. When they saw him from a distance, they could hardly recognize him; they began to weep aloud, and they tore their robes and sprinkled dust on their heads. Then they sat on the ground with him for seven days and seven nights. No one said a word to him, because they saw how great his suffering was." (Job 2:11-13 NIV)

I Must Keep Moving

When you are going through tough times in your life, it is important that you surround yourself with the right people. You must surround yourself with people who will comfort you in your time of distress, people who encourage you and build you up. You need to be surrounded by people who won't just say that they're praying for you but who will actually be there in times when you need them the most. Sometimes the comfort that someone needs isn't found in the words you say, but your presence alone can bring comfort. Never feel bad or condemn yourself because you can't find the words to say at the moment. Just sitting there in silence, your presence alone helps bring comfort and helps that someone to persevere.

Just last year, one of my spiritual brothers went through one of the most tragic events of his life. His mother died of cancer. I'll never forget turning around on stage during sound check for a chapel worship service and seeing my brother with tears in his eyes saying, "She's gone to be with the Lord. she's gone to be with Jesus." I was heartbroken because she was like a mom to me too. She loved Jesus and she loved her boys and husband so much. She loved people and was one of the sweetest people you'd ever meet. During that season, almost every day on my lunch break or right after work, I would go sit with my brother in his office, at his apartment, or at Starbucks, some days we would even go fishing.

Persevering with Integrity

Most days I had nothing to say, other days I would share with him revelation from God's word because we love to talk about the word together.

Never allow what the enemy does to you to push you into isolation. It is in the place of isolation that the enemy gains an advantage in your life. Even psychologists suggest that when people are depressed or grieving, they should force themselves to be around other people and that they should also force themselves to remain in places where there is a lot of light. The Bible says that God is light and in him is no darkness at all. The enemy desires to turn your heart against God and to cause you to become so overwhelmed by the circumstances you are experiencing that you not only push away from God but push away people in your life who carry the light of God.

I was there for my brother to comfort him in his time of need, while also observing how he persevered. Some days seemed good, some days were rough. I watched as he never blamed God. Not once did he say "God, you did this to me." Yes, he had questions and there were things he didn't understand, but he never allowed his unanswered questions to create a distaste for the Lord. Why, because he knew the heart of God. He continued to serve and worship while being broken. He had embraced the scripture in Psalm "The Lord is near to them of a broken heart." Sometimes it is in our season of brokenness that we are most aware of the nearness of God. When we are faced with difficulty, the presence of people matters, but the presence of God matters most. I watched my brother lean and become so dependent on the Lord in a way I had never seen anyone do in his situation.

> "How long will you torment me
> and crush me with words?
> Ten times now you have reproached me;
> shamelessly you attack me.
> If it is true that I have gone astray,
> my error remains my concern alone."
> -Job 19:2-4

Job was surrounded by friends who tried to be there for him, but they didn't understand his situation. Because they didn't understand, they developed assumptions and accusations about why he was experiencing such tragedy. They had developed the assumption that Job had sinned. Their assumption indicated their way of thinking. In their minds, trouble, and tragedy only happened in the lives of the wicked. Sometimes when people don't understand why you're going through what you're going through, they will make assumptions about what you're experiencing. The fact that his friends would question his character in this time of tragedy, could be an indication that his friends may not have

Persevering with Integrity

known him the way that they think they knew him. It is interesting that his own friends would call into question his character. Be careful of people who call into question your character when trouble hits your life, their opinion does more harm than help. It wasn't until his friends attempted to make sense of the situation that it made things worse. Sometimes we don't have the answer, and sometimes we don't know why people go through certain experiences, but we should never make assumptions that produce suggestions that don't help the situation.

Typically, when our character or integrity is called into question, our immediate reaction is to become defensive. In efforts to try and defend ourselves, sometimes we act out of character, therefore forfeiting our integrity for the sake of trying to convince people who refuse to believe that we are who we say we are.

Job was bitter, grieved, sorrowful, and even angry, yet he maintained his integrity. How? The fear of the Lord. **The fear of the Lord is how we maintain our integrity.** Without this one element, it is impossible for your integrity to remain intact when tragedy hits your life. What is the fear of the Lord? The fear of the Lord isn't being afraid of him, but it is having a great reverence for him.

"The fear of the Lord is to hate evil." **-Proverbs 8:13**

"The fear of the Lord is a fountain of life, that one may turn away from the snares of death." **-Proverbs 14:27**

The secret (intimacy) of the LORD is with those who fear him. He will show them his covenant. **-Psalm 25:14**

The reward for humility and fear of the Lord is riches and honor and life. **-Proverbs 22:4**

By mercy and truth iniquity is purged: and by the fear of the LORD men depart from evil. **-Proverbs 16:6**

It wasn't the fear of hell, man, or the devil that caused Job to maintain his integrity, but the fear (reverence) of the Lord. Even his wife couldn't understand how he could be facing such difficulty, yet maintain his integrity, and not curse God, "His wife said to him, "Are you still **maintaining your integrity**? Curse God and die!" (job 2:9) But Job was determined to continue to fear the Lord and maintain his integrity despite the happenings of life.

"Though he slay me, yet will I trust in him: but I will **maintain mine own ways** before him." **-Job 13:15**

Persevering with Integrity

"I will not remove **mine integrity** from me." **-Job 27:5**

    Life happens, and life will happen. We must not only keep people around us who help us stay grounded but there are certain elements that contribute to our ability to maintain our integrity in the face of difficulty. Decide today that regardless of what life throws at you, and no matter what the enemy does to you, you will continue to fear the Lord which will result in maintaining your integrity. Persevere with Integrity!

PRINCIPLES OF PERSEVERANCE

1. If you're going to successfully persevere in life, integrity is a key component.

2. When tragedy strikes, and circumstances arise, the condition of your heart is revealed.

3. Choose to worship; God's worth isn't determined by what he does or doesn't do, but who he is.

4. Never blame God for what the devil does.

5. Never allow the enemy to push you into isolation.

6. The fear (reverence) of the Lord is how we maintain our integrity.

7. Persevere with integrity!

Chapter 8
I'm going over

"On that day, when evening had come, He told them, "Let's cross over to the other side."
-Mark 4:35

When you know what God knows, you'll respond how he would respond in your shoes.

After Jesus' incredible yet challenging teaching on the parable of the sower, he initiates their next move. He says to his disciples, "Let us pass over unto the other side." The life that God has designed for you to live is never one-sided. Make up in your mind today that you won't settle with living a life that's one-sided. A life where you only see things one way just because that's all you've known. Just because you may be sick, broke, busted, and disgusted right now doesn't mean that's the side of life God wants you to live on.

I Must Keep Moving

He started it

"Let us go." This phrase suggests that Jesus was ready to move on to the next thing. "Let us" means that God wants to use you to be a part of what he's doing. I don't know about you, but I want to be wherever God is and a part of what he's doing. Have you gotten stuck in a certain place, mindset, or way of living and the Lord is ready to move on to the next thing? Can you discern when God is ready to make a move? God will never initiate a move in your life and he not go with you. There may be some people, old mindsets, and habits that can't go, but he'll never send you alone. Even Jesus in the book of John often spoke about the Father being with him "He that sent me is with me: The Father has not left me alone." As a child of God, I want you to know that God has not left you alone! It is his presence and grace that validates the move.

Sometimes it is our perception of ourselves and what others may think about us that makes us feel unqualified or unauthorized to make certain moves and complete certain tasks and assignments. Even Moses dealt with this issue in Exodus 3:11,12: "And Moses said unto God Who am I, that I should go unto Pharaoh, and that I should bring forth the children of Israel out of Egypt? And he said, Certainly I will be with you, and this shall be a sign that I have sent you." God understands that the success of your journey and God-given assignments is dependent upon his presence being with you. If he initiates a thing in your life, he's committed to what he starts and faithful to see it to completion. God wants to take you somewhere. Jesus didn't ask his disciples to follow him because he wanted an entourage, he wanted to show them that there was a life greater than the one they had been living. I wonder what God is trying to initiate in your life. I wonder where God is trying to take you but you've yet to simply say yes.

Don't go without him

Before Jesus initiated this move, he first ordained His 12 disciples that they would be with him, to preach, heal the sick, and cast out devils. He had given them authority, but they understood that operating in his authority meant remaining submitted to him. Jesus' disciples understood how vital it was to have his presence in their lives. When you truly value someone's presence, you are intentional about them being in your midst and you being in theirs. It says, "They took him even as he was in the ship."

Dismiss the crowd

I would like to briefly note that before they boarded the ship, they "sent away the multitudes." In other words, they dismissed the crowd. You're not truly on board with the next thing until you dismiss the "now" thing. The "now" thing is the thing that's kept you occupied up to this point and now you know you must dismiss it in order to go with God. You can't afford to be contained by the crowd. You must keep moving. Dismiss the crowd of uncertainty, the crowd of fear, the crowd of voices from your past, and even the crowd of people who praise you for being at your current level, but can not see you beyond where you are. Dismiss the crowd and board the ship. Lastly, don't try to bring people aboard the ship who weren't invited.

Here comes trouble

Encountering the storm was an indication that they were headed somewhere significant. Trouble on the shore isn't the same as trouble at sea. You can not expect to get to where God is calling you and not expect to go through anything. The Bible mentions 2 ways God responds to the trouble in our lives. Many are the afflictions of the righteous, but the Lord delivers him out of them all. Remember, the Lord is

I'm Going Over

a very present help in trouble. God will either deliver you from trouble immediately or get in it with you.

As much as God desires for us to value his presence, he desires that we have that same love for his principles. What Jesus teaches His disciples on one side gets tested by a storm. Trouble is used to test how firm we are in our belief of what we've been taught. Trouble sometimes has a way of creating confusion and uncertainty about the will of God. But I want you to know that there is nothing that you go through that would ever make God change his mind about the plans that he has for you. With God, Plan B is Plan A. Regardless of what comes and what goes, who stays, and who leaves, what you lose or what you gain, God's plans for you are still that you prosper and be in health as your soul prospers, and to give you hope and an expected end. Regardless of what things may look like right now, remind yourself of the expected end. What are you expecting? How are you expecting things to turn out in your marriage or your ministry? Do you expect to be single or broke for the rest of your life? When you continue to remind yourself of God's expected end for your life, it will empower you to persevere through the storms of life.

It's your cross-over season

Storms come to test the principles, not the presence. Jesus says that it is written, "Thou shall not tempt the Lord thy God." The power of what you hear is found in your understanding of it. You cannot expect fruit from what you simply hear but do not understand. "He that has an ear" is referring to your interest. Could it be that your lack of interest in understanding the principles and mysteries of God is affecting your endurance and ability to live a victorious life in Christ? One thing that I've learned, and I will continue to reiterate is that the devil gets an advantage in your life through what you don't know. It is our interest in hearing and understanding the principles of God that give us proper perspective and power over the storms of life.

No matter who we are or where we come from, none of us are exempt from experiencing the storms of life. Our storms may not all be the same, but the winds will blow and the seas will rage in your life. Whenever you're doing something significant, you can expect to experience some form of opposition. I believe the storms of life are sent by the enemy to hinder your progress and cloud your perception. He knows the more you progress and prosper, the more territory you take for the kingdom of God. That's what the storm in this text was about. It was about the territory that was on the other side.

I'm Going Over

The enemy knows that if he can get you to quit in the middle, you're not just forfeiting a successful future, you're forfeiting territory for the kingdom. Hell gets nervous when you give God your yes, because not only have you committed to journeying with God, but taking what rightfully belongs to you, from the enemy.

Don't jump ship

Notice how verse 36 is worded, "And there arose a great storm of wind." Did you catch it? A storm of wind. Wind is defined as a natural movement or current of air with velocity. It comes as no surprise that in Ephesians 2:2 the devil is called "the prince of the power of the air." According to Jewish opinion, the enemy and his demons fill the air. I firmly believe that this storm was sent by the devil himself as an attempt to hinder and ultimately stop the progress of Jesus and his disciples. On the other side was a man who was demon-possessed with unclean spirits, who lived in mountains and tombs, crying day and night, cutting himself with stones. The man on the other side needed the delivering power of Jesus Christ to set him free from the powers of darkness. The devil knew that the man's deliverance would cost him territory. Remember, this was not a breeze of wind they were experiencing, this was a wind that came in complete opposition to them, with speed. I've experienced several hurricanes and tropical storms in my life. I've even tried walking outside in a few of them, and the amount of wind pressure felt as if I would be blown away. I can only imagine the amount of wind pressure they experienced while on the ship.

Our connection to God is a ship. It's a relation**ship** and even on this ship we experience the storms of life. Not every day do we experience storms, but often when we are making significant moves and headed in the right direction, an opposing wind will come. Let that be encouragement to you, that just because you experience opposing winds, it doesn't mean you're doing something wrong or headed in the wrong direction.

Just as important as it is to cut off any negative relationships from your life, it is equally as important to maintain healthy ones. The pressures of life can cause you to neglect fellowship with God if you let them. There are times when you can become so stressed, frustrated, and anxious that you are too mentally, emotionally, and sometimes physically exhausted to pray, worship, praise, and read your bible. Choose now to change your perspective about the pressures of life and it will give you the ability to endure some of the most trying times.

Regardless of the storms that may hit your life, always remember that Jesus is on board. When the storm arose, and Jesus' disciples panicked, instead of

I'm Going Over

jumping ship in fear for their lives, they knew who to run to. When you're experiencing financial pressure, family pressure, ministry pressure, or any type of pressure in life, always run to Jesus. Why abandon your relationship with the one who has all power over whatever may oppose His will for your life? Don't abandon your relationship with the Lord, it is the most valuable thing you could ever possess on this earth.

Don't abandon your relationship with people. I know what it's like when the pressures of life are on, and you're so worried about bills, stressing over your health, overwhelmed with work, and it seems like things are falling apart in your family. In those moments, we are often tempted to go into isolation. When you jump ship, you are not only abandoning the one relationship that matters most, but you are also neglecting the relationships you have with people. Remember verse 36? "And there were also with him other little ships." Jesus and his disciples weren't the only ones experiencing the storm. Whenever you're experiencing the storms of life, always keep in mind that you're not the only one who's experiencing opposing winds and pressure. Don't allow the pressure and opposition to push you into isolation. When you are forced into isolation, you become an easy target for the enemy to destroy you. Stay connected to people, because they help you to endure through the storms of life.

In over your head

Have you ever said to yourself, "If it's not one thing, it's another," how about this, "things just can't get any worse"? Verse 37 says "and the waves beat into the ship, so that it was now full." The wind started affecting the waves. What they were above, now started to affect their ship. The wind may be the sickness in your body, and the waves may be the crazy medical bills, and now your relationship with God may be starting to waver and you are in question about his intentions for you. The enemy will always try to fill your ship with whatever he can to try and sink your ship so that you sink and drown. Always remember, when the winds are blowing, and the seas are raging, always run to Jesus.

Where's your faith?

Jesus' disciples ran to him in panic, yet they found him at peace. "And he was in the hinder part of the ship, asleep on a pillow: and they awake, and say unto him, Master, carest thou not that we perish" (Mark 4:38). Have you ever felt like God didn't care about what you were facing because he didn't respond the way that you thought he should? Because of what they experienced and their perspective, their conclusion was that they were going to die. That is what anxiety is, it is believing in

I'm Going Over

the worst possible outcome that has not happened. What you believe about God and yourself in comparison to what you see, will determine how you respond.

All of this is interesting because the book of Mark is a gospel that begins with an emphasis on the authority of Jesus' words.

"And they were astonished at His teaching, for He taught them as one having authority, and not as the scribes. Now there was a man in their synagogue with an unclean spirit. And he cried out, saying, "Let us alone! What have we to do with You, Jesus of Nazareth? Did You come to destroy us? I know who You are—the Holy One of God!" But Jesus rebuked him, saying, "Be quiet, and come out of him!" And when the unclean spirit had convulsed him and cried out with a loud voice, he came out of him. Then they were all amazed, so that they questioned among themselves, saying, "What is this? What new doctrine is this? For **with authority He commands** even the unclean spirits, and they **obey** Him." Mark (1:22-27)

When the disciples found Jesus, he was resting, he was at peace. Why? Because he understands that you don't panic about what you know you have authority over. Jesus said, "All power and authority has been given unto me, both in heaven and on earth." All power includes power over the prince of the power of the air. You see, the enemy gets an advantage in your life through what you don't know. "Lest Satan should get an advantage of us: for we are not ignorant of his devices." (2 Corinthians 2:11). Ignorance of who you are and what you possess will make you run from devils and circumstances you have power over.

    For years I've read this passage and assumed the issue was that the disciples had awakened Jesus out of his sleep until I realized, that wasn't the thing Jesus addressed. He asks them, "Why are you so fearful?" He addressed the fear in them. The storm didn't produce the fear, it revealed the fear. The storm revealed their lack of faith. They had fear that they would die, instead of faith that they would live. Their approach to Jesus revealed their perspective of the storm in comparison to who he is. His questioning of their fear and their faith suggests that after being with him for a while and seeing him operate by using the authority in his mouth, he expected them to have the faith and confidence that he could even calm a storm.

    Believe it or not, there is something that Jesus and this storm have in common. Do you know what that is? If you were to read this story in the King James Version of the Bible, you would find that it says, "And there *arose* a great storm of wind," and in verse 37 it says, "And he *arose*." I want you to know that God isn't afraid to stand up to what has you intimidated and scared. He's not afraid to confront what is causing chaos around you. When he stands up to the enemies of your life, purpose, marriage, business, ministry, etc., they must stand down. All power and authority are in the person and name of Jesus Christ.

Perspective

Here's what I've found to be very interesting. Notice carefully how Jesus deals with this storm. "And he arose, and **rebuked the wind** and **said to the sea**, Peace, be still." He didn't just say "Storm I rebuked thee," and there was a great calm. He addressed aspects of the storm in their proper context. In other words, he put things into perspective. The only reason that the sea was in an uproar was because of the raging winds. When God deals with your issue, he isn't interested in merely dealing with the symptoms, but getting to the root of your issue. God doesn't want to numb your pain, he wants to make you whole. He doesn't want you to have just temporary happiness, but eternal joy that is unspeakable and full of glory. Your perspective of the storms that happen in your life will determine how you respond to them.

I Must Keep Moving

For most of middle school and high school, I hated myself. I thought that if I had the clothes that the other students had, then I would like me. In my junior and senior years of High School, I was able to afford the clothes that the other students could afford, I felt good about myself for a while, but soon that wore away. I quickly realized that I still didn't like me. Why? Because there was no external solution for an internal issue. I had an internal storm called low self-esteem. The issue was with how I saw myself inwardly. What am I saying? Sometimes we think that the issue is one thing when it's only the symptom of another. The symptom was that I didn't like myself, but the root was I didn't esteem myself. How did I cause this internal storm to cease? I did it by saying, "Low self-esteem, I rebuke thee!" No... Of course not! You can't rebuke low self-esteem away by just saying "I rebuke thee!" Wouldn't it be awesome if we could do that for everything? However, I did rebuke the low self-esteem, but not the way you would do a devil. How did I do it? I did it by esteeming myself with truth. Remember, Jesus says "Father, your word is truth." Jesus also says, "You shall know the truth, and the truth shall make you free." You must face your storms with truth. Truth stood up to this storm in Mark 5. How do I know? Jesus says, "I am the way, **the truth**, and the life."

I'm Going Over

The raging wind was the root and the roaring sea was the symptom. **Remember, Jesus was at peace within himself. The power of internal peace is that it affords you the capacity to properly perceive external problems and deal with them correctly.** The way he dealt with the wind isn't the same way he dealt with the sea. He was careful not to rebuke the sea. He understood that the sea was essential to him reaching his destination. Never allow the storms and chaos around you to cause you to disapprove of the things or people you need for your journey. The family member or friend whom you love so dearly may be experiencing wind pressure and it could be affecting their actions, but don't allow it to cause you to treat them like an enemy. Remember, "For we wrestle not against flesh and blood, but against principalities, against powers, against the rulers of the darkness of this world, against spiritual wickedness in high places" (Ephesians 6:12).

None of us willingly invite the storms of life. As chaotic and disturbing as the may be, God uses storms as an opportunity to give us a revelation of himself that we didn't already have. Jesus' disciples responded, "What **manner** of man is this, that *even* the wind and the sea obey him?" Their response/question suggests that they were very much aware of his authority, but they had never seen it on that level and in that type of situation. The

I Must Keep Moving

revelation of God that you gain in the midst of a storm is what becomes the fuel that you need to keep moving!

I'm Going Over

PRINCIPLES OF PERSEVERANCE

1. Don't settle for living on one level.

2. If God initiates anything in your life, he's committed to what he starts and faithful to see it to completion.

3. You're not truly on board with the next thing until you dismiss the now thing.

4. When you continue to remind yourself of God's expected end for your life, it will empower you to persevere through the storms of life.

5. If you quit, you forfeit territory, and your future.

6. Opposing winds don't mean you're doing something wrong or headed in the wrong direction. The wind opposition is often from the enemy who's threatened and intimidated by your progress.

7. Never abandon your relationships with the right people. Remember, you're not the only one who experiences storms.

8. Internal peace affords you the capacity to properly perceive external problems and deal with them correctly.

9. The revelation of God that you gain in the midst of a storm is what becomes the fuel you need to keep moving.

Chapter 9
Move on

"Move on." A phrase that is often easier said than done. Whether it's moving on from the loss of a loved one, a divorce, a breakup, or even a failure, moving on can be one of the most difficult things to do. Many of us have met people who have gone through many obstacles in life and have overcome them. Often, it is those same people who find us in similar situations and their simple advice, with the purest of intentions, maybe "move on." It is not that they are insensitive to what we are facing. I believe that sometimes we may forget how difficult it was for us in one season to move on. Moving on may sound like a simple fix, but often is no easy process.

What do you have to lose? Forget what's behind.

I Must Keep Moving

Forgetting isn't denial. Forgetting isn't ignoring what happened. It is releasing things that aren't assets to what's up ahead. Paul was a man who was zealous of the things of the law. He could be considered the top of his class. He was passionate about the Jewish religion. In fact, he was so passionate that he persecuted Christians to the point of death. The Jewish religion was everything to Paul. He called himself "a Hebrew of the Hebrews." "Touching the righteousness which is in the law, blameless." Paul prided himself on his accomplishments as a Pharisee. However, after he encountered Christ, that all changed for him. He says, "But what things were gain to me, those I counted loss for Christ." What may be keeping you from moving on could be an unwillingness to let go of the things that are gain to you.

I teach at a Christian school and every Monday I take most of the class time to teach a devotion from the verse of the week. One week our verse was 1 Corinthians 13:4,5 "Love is patient, and is kind; it does not envy, it does not boast, it is not arrogant, it is not rude. it is not self-seeking, it is not easily provoked, it keeps no record of wrong." To see the look on the students' faces, after reading this verse, was absolutely priceless. I knew immediately what that meant. As most of us have already done, my students had their own definition of love that they had developed on the basis of their experiences.

Move on!

One conviction that I strongly live by is that the moment we encounter truth, we are forced to make a decision. We either change what we believe or continue down our own path. When we first encounter truth, it rubs us the wrong way to bring discomfort and test the validity and strength of how we think or believe. Truth will interrupt your normal to invite you into a better quality of life. The invitation can be declined by an unwillingness to let go of a certain way of thinking or believing and embrace God's word which then governs how we think and believe.

I shared this conviction I live by with all my students so that they could see that it was time to make a decision. I knew that if they continued to live by an ungodly definition of love, then it would affect their ability to move on in life. Like most scriptures, parts of these verses were very challenging for most of my students, especially the part about keeping no record of wrong.

I took a survey in each one of my classes and asked them several questions about these verses. One of the questions I asked them was, "Why do we like to keep a record of other people's wrongs that they do to us?" The common answer that I found in each one of my classes was that it makes them feel good to know that they have something to hold over the offender's head. Then it hit me! People have a hard time forgiving because they think that as long as they hold on to the offense it will make the person who hurt them hurt as much as they are hurting. This, my friend, is far from the truth. To most people, unforgiveness is gain to them. Unforgiveness isn't killing the one who offended or hurt you, it's slowly killing you. Many people are physically sick because of unforgiveness. I even had a student come up to me after the class, and she told me that she had been feeling sick and suffering from shortness of breath. She shared with me that as I was talking about forgiveness, God had revealed to her the source of her illness, unforgiveness. This isn't a book about forgiveness, however, I do want to give you several keys to begin your process to ultimately forgiving someone whom you've yet to forgive. Unforgiveness hinders your ability to keep moving. Time will go on, you will grow old, yet still lack progress if you don't forgive. I don't want that for you, and neither should you! I want to see you progress, and live a whole and fulfilling life.

"Moving on isn't about mere movement, but it is about healthy progression."

1. Forgiveness is a decision. It's up to you to let it go, not them. Whether you choose to let it go or not, doesn't affect the offender.
2. The people who broke you aren't responsible for fixing you.

Move on!

3. "They" owe you nothing in order for you to forgive. (I shared with my students the sad reality that some apologies you may never get. Some people don't believe that they've done anything wrong, and no matter how much you cry, kick, scream, post on social media, or even try to tarnish their reputation, you still may never get them to admit they're wrong and give you an apology.)
4. The power of forgiveness is not in their actions, it's in your decision!
5. Pray

Get up

In John 5, Jesus encounters a man who had an infirmity for 38 years. John does not give us a background story of the invalid's condition like he does the blind man in John 9. We aren't told if he was born ill or not, but what I would dare to suggest is that because we are given a time frame, he was not born an invalid, this happened over time. Had the man been born this way, the writer John would've clearly stated it just as he did in regards to the blind man in John 9:1 where he says "And as Jesus passed by, he saw a man which was blind from his birth."

The invalid's condition was something that happened to him. Where he had ended up, he was not alone, there were other people in this place called

I Must Keep Moving

Bethesda as well. People who were impotent, blind, halted, withered. One thing that they all had in common is that they were all waiting for the **moving** of the water. Different conditions, and different needs, all waiting for the same source of wholeness. Every season this man missed his chance to be made whole. He just couldn't seem to get to the pool fast enough. There was always someone who was a step ahead of him. Have you ever felt like you've missed your season? Have you ever felt like everyone else was always a step ahead of you? Like you didn't have what it took to get there fast enough? It can be a frustrating thing when you don't feel like you have it in you to do what others have done to get the breakthrough they've gotten. The man lies there waiting for people to put him in what everyone else is stepping into. If he knew that everyone was always a step ahead of him, the smart thing to do would've been to somehow get a head start. While he's lying there, Jesus walks up and asks the man, "Do you want to be whole? It seems like the obvious answer would be, yes, considering the man's reason for being there in the first place, until you realize what Jesus was looking for. When you notice the word choice in his question, then you see what he was after. Jesus was looking for desire.

Most people have preached and taught that this man begins to give Jesus excuses. Personally, I believe he was only sharing with Jesus his

Move on!

experience, which brings me back to Jesus' question. I believe that Jesus was asking this man, "For all that you have experienced, is there still a desire in you to be made whole?"

To my reader, I know people probably weren't there for you the way you thought they should've been. Maybe the people you thought you would do life with have walked away. Maybe the guy or girl you thought would bring you happiness and wholeness has let you down. I have one question for you: for all the disappointment you may have experienced up to this point, is there still a desire in you to be whole? Is there still a desire in you to love again, trust again, or believe again? Let today be the day you stop allowing what did or didn't happen to you or for you to speak up when it's time for your breakthrough!

Jesus didn't waste any time entertaining the man's experience. Not because Jesus was insensitive, but because he understood that the man's past experiences had no bearing on his wholeness. As long as you're waiting for the person who offended you to come back and apologize, you are prolonging your wholeness. Often it is what we choose to entertain that keeps us stuck. Had Jesus entertained what people did or didn't do for the man, it would've turned into gossip and a blame game. You must keep moving! Remember, your destiny is too great, and your purpose is too valuable for you to miss your moment to be whole again because of disappointment with people you expected too much out of.

Jesus spoke to the man and said "Rise, take up your bed, and walk." He was immediately made whole, took up his bed, and walked. Note that the first thing Jesus told him to do was rise, and the man arose. He didn't just rise because he was made whole, he made a decision to rise. Even after he was made whole, he could've decided to continue to lay there because of how comfortable the bed was. Jesus' command, "Rise, take up your bed, and walk," gives us a principle of how God desires us to handle wholeness. He doesn't make us whole for us to be lazy and comfortable, but he desires that we own our wholeness. If I were to paraphrase Jesus' command, I would say that he told this man to "rise, take up your bed, and move on." It's time for you to move on! It's time for you to move on from yesterday's disappointment. It's time to move on from the comfort of living less than whole. You weren't created to sit idle and watch life pass you by. Remember, you were created for so much more than mere survival. Sometimes God will allow people to overlook you and overstep you just so that he can get the glory out of your breakthrough. You may feel forgotten or overlooked, but I want you to know that God sees you right where you are, and knows how long you've been in the condition you're in. You may

Move on!

have missed stepping into your season in the past, but when God shows up, he comes to give you a new season. He comes to help you get moving and to keep you moving.

After the man was made whole, he started moving as he was commanded to. Once he started moving, he started being criticized by the Jews saying, "It is the sabbath day: it is not lawful for you to carry your bed." Remember, when you start making moves don't be surprised when you start getting criticized by people who are so bound by a system of thinking and believing that your movement makes them uncomfortable. They asked him who it was that made him whole, at first, he had no clue, then after a second encounter with the Son of God, the man responds, "It was Jesus." God is going to do something so monumental in your life that only he will get the glory, and the only thing you will be able to tell people is, "It was Jesus!" Here's what this man has in common with Paul, if this man was going to step into a new season, then he had to forget the bad experience of people not meeting his exceptions, embrace his desire, and make a decision to obey the command, and move on.

You're coming out

One thing that is always important for you to keep in mind is that God has the best in mind for you.

I Must Keep Moving

The children of Israel were forced into slavery by the Egyptians, yet God had incredible plans for their lives. The bondage, oppression, and affliction weren't enough to stop what God had purposed in his heart for His children. You must get that in your heart immediately, that no matter what the devil does or how miserable he tries to make your life, God has incredible plans for your life. Remember the promise that God made to Abraham concerning his seed?

"Then the Lord said to him: 'Know for certain that for four hundred years your descendants will be strangers in a land that is not their own and that they will be enslaved and mistreated there. But I will punish the nation they serve as slaves, and afterward, **they will come out** with great possessions." (Genesis 15:13,14)

On that day the Lord made a covenant with Abram and said, "To your descendants, I give this land. Genesis 15:18

In Exodus 3:8, God speaks to Moses and says, "So I have come down to rescue them from the hand of the Egyptians and **to bring them up out** of that land into a good and spacious land, a land flowing with milk and honey—the home of the Canaanites, Hittites, Amorites, Perizzites, Hivites, and Jebusites."

Move on!

The will of God is not that you stay in bondage. It is not God's desire that you stay in a place or season that he has not ordained for you. He will do whatever it takes to get you moving to the place he has destined for you to be.

When Israel cried, God remembered His covenant. Before they had a problem, God already had a solution that came in the form of a promise. I firmly believe that when their cry of wanting out, matched with God's plan and desire to bring them out, it provoked God to make a move. Most times it's not until you're tired of being where you are and what you're in that causes God to respond to deliver you. The children of Israel were living in Egypt, benefitting from the favor of Joseph. After Joseph died, a Pharaoh arose who did not know Joseph, and that's when the oppression and affliction began. It is unfortunate that they had to experience such harsh living conditions, but I believe the affliction was necessary to get them moving. Remember, Egypt was not the land that God promised. They were in a land that was not their own. Sometimes God's way of getting you to what's yours is by making you uncomfortable where are. He is a God who knows how to get you moving. He doesn't want you to live a life less than the one he has planned and promised you. Joseph was a representation of favor, eventually, he died. God will cause the favor in a place to expire as an indication that it's time to make a move. You are probably wondering how is it that after 10 years of everything going so well on your job, now it seems like there's more drama than ever, and you've done nothing, yet you somehow find yourself in the middle of it. You are caught in the middle of other people's agenda and now it seems like they're trying to make your life miserable because they recognize your potential and how blessed you are, and it intimidates them. Pharaoh was intimidated and he felt threatened, but his attitude was necessary in creating that kind of discomfort that would cause the children of Israel to cry unto the Lord. When they cried, God raised up a deliverer named Moses. Moses was a Hebrew who was raised as an Egyptian. I won't go much into detail about his life experiences or his encounter with God, but here are two thoughts I have gathered from their exit.

1. God will be honored and glorified upon any enemy that opposes your movement or progress towards your promise.

2. God will take care of the obstacles that are before you and the enemies that are behind you.

When the children of Israel departed from Egypt, they were pursued by Pharaoh and his army.

Move on!

Immediately, the children of Israel began to talk out of their fears: "And they said unto Moses, 'Was it because there were no graves in Egypt that you brought us to the desert to die? What have you done to us by bringing us out of Egypt? Didn't we say to you in Egypt, 'Leave us alone: let us serve the Egyptians'? It would have been better for us to serve the Egyptians than to die in the desert. Exodus 14:11,12

Sometimes what we think is best for us isn't what God thinks is best for us. Their words were a reflection of a conclusion they had already developed in their minds. God tells Moses to speak to them and tell them to move on: "Then the Lord said to Moses, 'Why are you crying out to me? Tell the Israelites to **move on**." Don't worry about what's chasing you! Remember, you've got goodness and mercy following you. Keep moving and God will fight for you. Soon he will drown out the enemies of your past. No longer will you live in anxiety and fear of an enemy catching up with you. You don't have time to be paralyzed by fear and assuming the worst. God has never lost a battle! Stand still and see the Salvation of the Lord.

I Must Keep Moving

You're Not Going To Die

One of the hardest things to do is trust someone when you don't know their intentions. Moses knew that God's heart towards the children of Israel was nothing but good. It's easy to assume that because they had experienced God's protection, they would have the faith to trust God for provision. When God is trying to disconnect you from certain things or people who have always been your source, it can be difficult to adapt. Egypt's culture was the norm to the children of Israel although they were slaves to it. God's people were used to having food, water, clothing, and shelter right at their fingertips. There was no need for faith for provision, it was supplied by their enemies. God is a jealous God when it comes to his children, and he refuses to allow his enemies to be what he exists to be in your life.

Remember, as a result of the Egyptians increasing the burdens and intensifying the labor of God's children, they cried to God, and he heard them, and raised up a deliver. How encouraging! God will never ignore the cry of His children. It doesn't matter the bondage, depression, oppression, sickness, sin, or condition you may be in, God is able and willing to deliver you from the enemy! Many are the afflictions of the righteous, but the Lord delivers him out of them all! God is faithful to get you OUT! I believe that this is your coming out season! You're

Move on!

coming out of guilt, out of debt, out of depression, out of sickness, out of shame! You're coming out!

Whenever God wants to get something done on the earth, he'll find and use somebody. When God's children CRIED, he made a CALL! He called and chose Moses. After Moses dealt with his moment of inadequacy and approached Pharaoh numerous times about letting God's people go, God showed his mighty power and helped his children to escape. I love that God kept instructing Moses to go to Pharaoh, that tells me that God will not give up on getting you out! God will never give up on your freedom! I feel that today is a day of freedom for someone who's reading this right now. God loves you, and he wants what's best for you!

God brought the children of Israel out, not just to bring them out, but so that they could hold a feast and worship him! The greatest response you could give God when he delivers you is worship and communion (fellowship) with the Holy Spirit.

In Exodus 16:3 it says, "The Israelites said to them, 'If only we had died by the LORD's hand in Egypt! There we sat around pots of meat and ate all the food we wanted, but you have brought us out into this desert to starve this entire assembly to death.'" I can almost sympathize with the children of Israel's anxiety because they were trying to follow a God whom they did not know intimately, but Moses their leader did. Moses knew God's intentions, but they didn't. God has disconnected them from a system they were dependent on and now they are trying to adapt to a new system. To them this was a crisis, therefore they murmured and complained.

Murmuring and complaining reveal 3 things:
1. You haven't learned the heart and intentions of God toward you.
2. You need to adapt more to God's system.
3. You're allowing what you see/don't see and feel to determine your response towards God when you don't understand.

Sometimes God uses a crisis to introduce you to his kingdom system that is lived by faith. In Egypt, they saw how things were going to be provided, in the wilderness they had to learn the heart of God to trust him by faith that he would provide everything they needed! God's intention wasn't that they would die, but that they would live, BY FAITH! Often when we don't have what we need, when we think we need it or can't see where it's coming from, it feels like we're going to "die," like it's the end of our world and sometimes that's what we tell ourselves! "It's over, I'm finished, I knew this was too good to be true, way to go, God, etc." I want to encourage you today, it may feel like it, and it may look like God isn't going to come through, but just know that you're not going

Move on!

to die, so keep moving! There are amazing promises over your life! God always keeps his promises! His kingdom lifestyle is designed to bless you and keep you moving!

I Must Keep Moving

PRINCIPLES OF PERSEVERANCE

1. What may be keeping you from moving on could be an unwillingness to let go of the things that are gain to you.

2. Truth interrupts your "normal" to invite you into a better quality of life.

3. Moving on isn't about mere movement, but healthy progression.

4. As long as you're waiting for the person who offended you to come back and apologize, you are prolonging your wholeness.

5. Sometimes God will allow people to overlook you and overstep you just so that he can get the glory out of your breakthrough.

6. One decision coupled with desire can shift the season of your life.

7. Sometimes God's way of getting you to what's yours, is by making you uncomfortable where you are.

Move on!

8. God is committed to getting you out of where you aren't meant to be and getting you to the place he wants you to be.

9. Move on!

CHAPTER 10
Get a head

If you don't get "a head," you won't get ahead. In other words, if you don't learn how to control your thinking and have the right mindset, then it will affect your ability to either get moving or keep moving. I wrote this book to inspire and empower you to persevere, and I would do you a great disservice if I didn't give you principles and write to you about the importance and the power of the mind when it comes to perseverance. My spiritual father always says, "If you don't quit, then you can't be stopped." Often, it is not the circumstances that surround us that tempt us to quit, it is most times our thinking.

Why you need "a head"
"But as one was felling a beam, the axe head fell into the water; and he cried out and said, 'Alas, my master! For it was borrowed." **-2 Kings 6:5**

I Must Keep Moving

The mind is one of the most powerful things a human being possesses. It is because of the human mind that many contributions have been and are made to the evolution and progress of our society. Thinking people have provided innovative solutions for crises in the world in which we live. The desire of God is that we use the mind according to the intention in which he created it, for productivity and governance. Much like one of the sons of the prophets who lost the ax head, without a mind, there'll be a lot of motion, but no productivity. You are a tool and the most important part of who you are is your head. To lose your head is to lose your ability to persevere and progress.

"I am not what I feel"

I repeat this to myself every day of my life. "I am not what I feel." Now I'm telling you, you are NOT what you feel. What you feel is very much real, but it does not have to govern your actions and mental state. Most studies and research present you with the notion that males aren't very emotional. I can only speak for myself when I say that until around my mid-20s, I have always been a very emotional individual. Growing up, this is what kept me in the principal's office, getting suspended from school, and even "the rod of correction" from my parents. I've always acted on what I felt. Over time, this way of living became dangerous for me to the point where I ended up in an addiction and cycle that took 10 years to break. Living by what I felt was so unhealthy that it even started to affect my relationships and how I handled breakups. I can remember praying to God almost every night, "Please God, please help me to control my emotions. Why am I so emotional? Why do I allow what I feel to govern my actions?" I wanted out so bad, but I had no idea how to get free. Living by what I felt started affecting my prayer life. The time I would spend with the Lord became the time I gave to the addiction. It had become so much about feelings to me, that is what I began to base God's presence off of. If I didn't feel him, I assumed he had left me. I had made my feelings and emotions my god.

    I can remember one day coming across a sermon on YouTube by Kenneth Hagin. I can't remember the title of his sermon, but what I do remember him saying is "Most people base their relationship with God and his presence off of what they feel. Friend, this is a very shallow and sensual way to live as a believer. Your feelings can't be trusted. Your feelings will lie to you and say God's not with you when His word tells you in 1 John 3:24 and 1 John 4:13 that he dwells in you by his Spirit which he has given to us." I'll never forget how liberating that moment was for me. Kenneth Hagin gave life-changing instructions in that message, and he told the congregation to declare those scriptures whenever they don't feel like God is there. I suddenly realized that believers don't walk by sight or what we feel, but we walk by faith! The scripture had become real to me. I then understood that the presence of God was meant to be known rather than felt.

A layer of sensuality had been lifted off of me. To this day, I still declare those verses over my life every morning. Not only am I giving myself a daily reminder of the truth that He's in me and with me, but it heightens my awareness of Him. I knew God was with me, in me, and I knew he was enough, but it still seemed as if I was missing something. I knew deep within myself that there was something that I didn't know either about God or myself that would grant me the freedom that I so desperately longed for. I constantly prayed, "Lord show me, show me what I'm missing. I want to be free from my feelings and emotions controlling my life."

To find what I desperately longed for, I gave myself to the word of God, prayer, and fasting. During my time of intense searching for freedom, I read two books of the bible that completely changed my life forever, Romans and Galatians. I soon began to realize, it was what I didn't know that was affecting my ability to persevere. I always felt and lived under so much guilt, shame, and condemnation. I lived my life as a child of God,

Get A Head

feeling worthless, insecure, not good enough, and feeling like God was never pleased with me. I lived under the assumption that God was never pleased with me to the point where I thought to myself, Why bother? Why even try to live for God if I can never get it right anyway? I remember saying to myself, "If I'm going to hell, then I may as well go live it up." Do you see what was happening? I was about to turn away from God because I felt guilt, shame, and condemnation, and I felt like God was never pleased with me. This is exactly what Satan wants you do to. He will do whatever it takes to get you to walk away from God, even if it means getting you to believe a doctrine that makes think you have to earn your Salvation. My friend, any kind of teaching/preaching that makes you believe you have to earn your salvation, or that God is never pleased with you, and makes you condemn yourself, it is demonic. You will always feel like you'll never measure up and like you're destined for hell.

As you can see, my world was chaotic because I was missing one thing, a renewed mind. I didn't just need any kind of mind, I needed the mind of Christ. I needed His head. I was having a hard time getting ahead because I didn't have his head. Paul says, "Be transformed by the renewing of your mind." I asked the question to myself, "What kind of mind do I need to have?" I know it needs to be renewed, but what does that look like? I came across this scripture in

I Must Keep Moving

Romans 8:6 "To be carnally minded is death; but to be spiritually minded is life and peace." After reading this verse, I knew immediately why I lived a life as a believer, void of peace. Peace isn't a feeling, it is harmony between your mind and spirit. To be carnally minded or fleshly minded means that I allow how I feel to determine how I think; to be spiritually minded means that I allow the voice of the Holy Spirit and God's word to govern my thinking. That's the kind of mind that Jesus had, a spiritual mind. Romans 8:7 says, "Because the carnal mind is hostile against God: for it is not subject to the law of God, neither indeed can be." The word *law* in this verse means, "Force and influence that persuades to action." There is a kind of thinking that resists God's influence, but that kind of thinking only leaves you void of peace, and separated from experiencing the kind of life God desires you to live. The Holy Spirit should be the greatest voice of influence in your life. If he doesn't have your ear, he may not completely have your heart. Having the Head (mind) of Christ means that your thinking is in agreement with God's word and the influence of the Holy Spirit.

My goal here isn't to give a theological discourse, but I want to give you the truth that has set me free and continues to help me persevere in my faith. I'm about to help you get a head!

Get A Head

Romans 8:1 "There is therefore now no condemnation to them who are in Christ Jesus." Condemnation means "to be worthy of punishment." It's important for you to know that because of the shed blood of Jesus Christ, the wrath of God is not coming upon His children (see Romans 5:9). Walking around in condemnation is like constantly telling yourself "God hates me, and he's going to punish me."

Romans 5:1 "Therefore being justified by faith, we have peace with God through our Lord Jesus Christ." The word justified here means "to be declared righteous; or to be made right with God." You are made right God, and on God's "good side" through what Jesus Christ has done on the cross of Calvary.

Remember the really bad addiction I had? Remember how I felt like I couldn't get free from living according to my feelings? Well, I discovered something during the period of intense consecration. I came across Galatians 5:16-25:

"I say then: Walk in the Spirit, and you shall not fulfill the lust of the flesh. For the flesh lusts against the Spirit, and the Spirit against the flesh; and these are contrary to one another, so that you do not do the things that you wish. But if you are led by the Spirit, you are not under the law. Now the works of the flesh are evident, which are: adultery, fornication, uncleanness, lewdness, idolatry, sorcery, hatred, contentions, jealousies, outbursts of wrath, selfish ambitions, dissensions, heresies, envy, murders, drunkenness, revelries, and the like; of which I tell you beforehand, just as I also told you in time past, that those who practice such things will not inherit the kingdom of God. But the fruit of the Spirit is love, joy, peace, longsuffering, kindness, goodness, faithfulness, gentleness, and self-control. Against such there is no law. And those who are Christ's have crucified the flesh with its passions and desires. If we live in the Spirit, let us also walk in the Spirit."

    It was at that moment that my life changed forever. I realized that I had gone about trying to gain control over living according to my feelings and fleshly desires all wrong. For me, it was grit my teeth and try not to do what I felt, which only further robbed me of power. The bible doesn't teach me to <u>try</u> not to fulfill the lust or evil, corrupt, and intense desires of my flesh, it instructs me to walk in the Spirit and I won't fulfill the lust of my flesh. Walking in the Spirit is very simple. Remember, repentance is abandoning your own way of thinking and embracing and agreeing with God's ways and thoughts. That's how you walk in the Spirit and the by-product is power over what you feel. You're not what you feel, you're a child of God. Change the way you think by submitting your mind to the law (force and influence) of God and you will gain power over your feelings, the opinions of people, and the voice of Satan.

Get A Head

Changing the way you think isn't done just by reading, praying, and heeding God's word. I want to also give you some more practical ways you can change the way you think. The more you expose your brain to new stimuli, over and over, it will eventually adjust and adapt to what you are exposing it to. Expose yourself to new environments, information, and even people. By exposing yourself to new things, you choose to break your routine. Your routine can only give you a cycle of results and your brain won't have anything new to adjust to. Challenge your brain by breaking your routine. Your worldview was never meant to be determined and limited to where you were born and raised. By changing the way you think through exposing yourself to new things, people, and places, you expand your capacity. What you think about, and what you expose yourself to, matters to God. With the help and guidance of the Holy Spirit, he will filter your mind and warn you of things that aren't safe and pure, and that are counterproductive to changing your mind for the better.

Decide today to give yourself to the word of God and prayer on another level. May your routine be broken and may you be exposed to greatness that provokes your mind to think differently. It's time for you to get "a head," so that you can get ahead! The journey is too great for you to lose your head! May God give you a mind to persevere!

PRINCIPLES OF PERSEVERANCE

1. Your mindset affects your ability to persevere

2. You are not what you feel.

3. Change your thinking through the word of God, prayer, and breaking your routine.

4. God lives in you by his Spirit.

5. A mind in agreement with the word and Spirit of God gives us power over our flesh.

6. Peace is when your mind and spirit are in harmony.

7. Exposing yourself to new things and people helps to change the way you think and empowers you to persevere.

As I conclude this book, I pray that you have been, not only inspired but empowered to persevere!

I declare that no longer will your feelings control your thinking and your actions. No longer will you live out of control, making irrational decisions because of how you feel in the moment. May you be free from all guilt, shame, condemnation, and ignorance that could be affecting your ability to progress and persevere. May you develop the courage and fortitude to make "God moves." May your latter days be greater than your former. I declare that you will break generational curses in your family, and open a door of generational blessings through your faith and obedience. I declare that you will be confident, and certain of who you are and what you carry. Whenever life happens, may you never lose your integrity, and blame God for what the devil does. May you no longer be delayed, manipulated, and controlled by the words and emotions of people who misunderstand you. I declared that you will fill the earth with God's glory and express, establish, and expand his kingdom in the earth. May it not be by might, nor by power, but by the Spirit of God! When you are faced with unexpected circumstances, in over your head, or tempted to quit, may the Spirit of God rise up in you to tell yourself, "I MUST KEEP MOVING!"

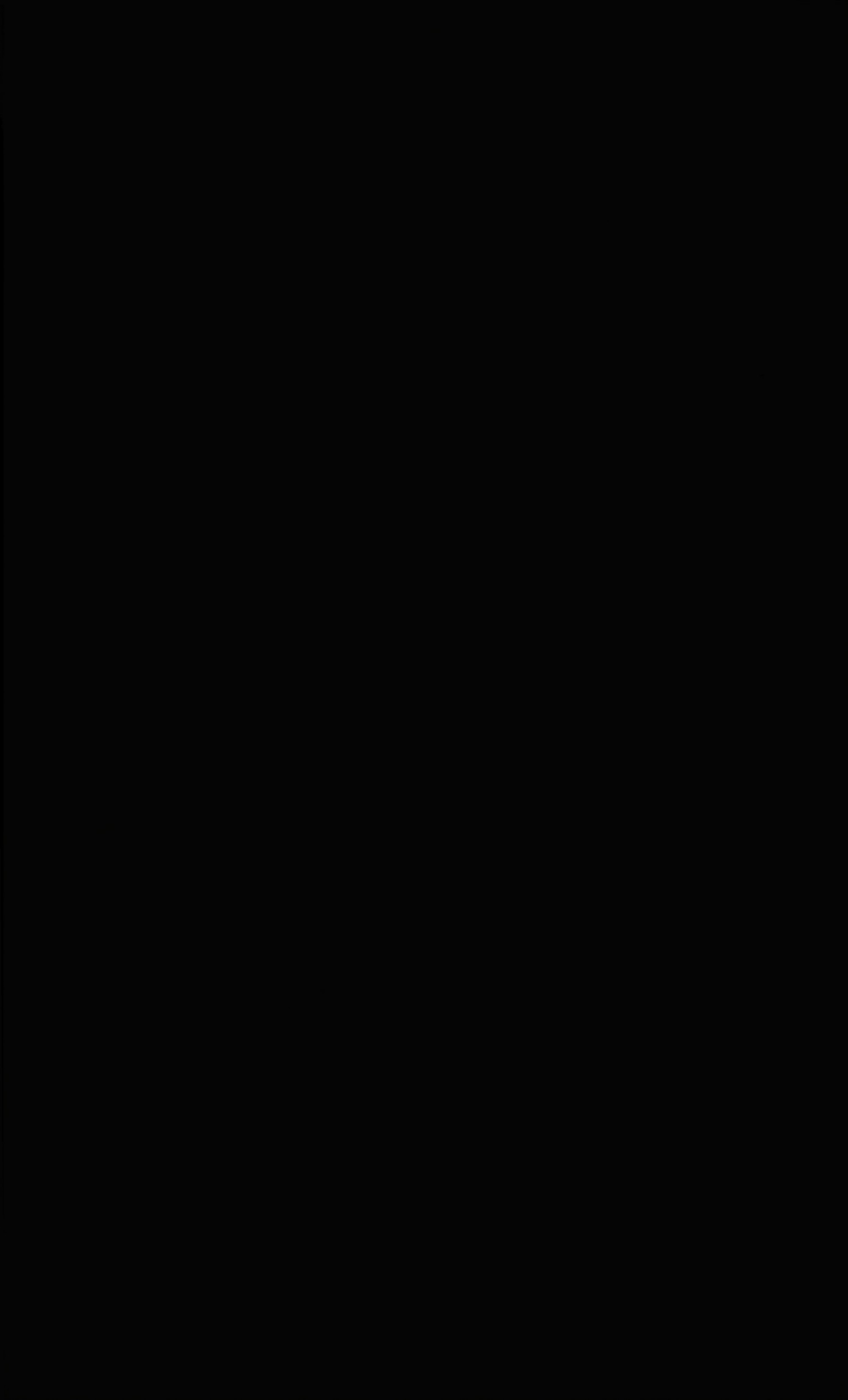

www.ingramcontent.com/pod-product-compliance
Lightning Source LLC
Chambersburg PA
CBHW020418080526
44584CB00014B/1386